HUNGARIAN REVIEW

Volume IV., No. 4. July 2013

CONTENTS

ARTS AND LITERATURE

On the cover: The Memorial of Transylvanian Prince Ferenc Rákóczi II. The outer wall of St Elisabeth's Cathedral, Kassa (Košice, Slovakia). An illustration to *Comrade Baron* by Jaap Scholten. Photo by Róbert Szebeni Szabó.

MAKING VOTERS COUNT

Editorial Note by John O'Sullivan

In the relatively brief interval since our last issue, there have been riots and disturbances of a more or less political kind in Turkey, Brazil and Egypt. These riots are separated by periods of three years or less from similar outbursts of popular discontent in London and Manchester, Tunisia, Libya, Bahrain, and Egypt again. And smaller or at least less noticed disturbances have taken place elsewhere – in France, in Greece, in Sweden.

Three years ago these events were seen as a localised or culturally distinct phenomenon: the Arab/Islamic Spring. They were also viewed through a certain lens as strivings towards more accountable government. That explanation served in effect as a justification: oppressed peoples rightly seeking to be democratic as the 19th century British statesman, W. E. Gladstone might have described them. So what are we to make of the three most recent disturbances in countries that are undeniably, if imperfectly, democratic by the clearest test: elections following which power changed hands.

Doubtless each national case is different. Nor do we know how any of them will turn out. At the time of writing a coup is taking place in Cairo; it might yet become a civil war. In addition to examining the particulars, however, we should surely ask whether or not there is some general phenomenon taking place before our eyes: a multicultural imitation of the 1848 or 1919 revolutions perhaps.

Professor İlter Turan's dispassionate and precise dissection of the events in Istanbul seems to raise that possibility, especially when his analysis is set alongside reports of the Brazilian riots. After pointing out that the demonstrators in Gezi Park were drawn from different religious and social groups, but that they were generally civic-minded, mutually respectful and mutually protective, he hazards the theory that a new political animal is emerging in Turkish life: "the socially engaged individual citizen who expects a government to be open to regular communications with citizens, more responsive to citizen preferences, and more respectful of the individual's privacy. Expressed differently, they want more refined democratic governance: limited not interventionist, pluralistic not monistic, inclusionary not exclusionary".

Except that they were more violent – not a trivial difference, of course – most of the Brazilian rioters seem to fit into a similar social-cum-ideological framework. Neither set of rioters is what we usually mean by "extremists". It is a comforting, even encouraging, picture. But the demands of both sets of rioters are still more extreme – well, more "problematic" – than they sound.

Democracy operates on the principle that the majority party forms a government and determines policy. Consultation, criticism and loyal opposition are part of the democratic package too – the liberal part. And a wise government will generally abstain from laws that intrude needlessly into people's lives. But sometimes deep disagreements exist; unavoidably one side will win and another lose; and choices have to be made. Until now it has been generally agreed that political debate ends eventually and the majority gets its way until the next election. Has that changed?

If we are to depart from this model, as critics of merely "majoritarian democracy" sometimes seem to suggest (and as some rioters implicitly demand), then we will be moving to a different political system. It may be that this system will prove to be more pluralist, more flexible, more inclusionary – and, for all those reasons, more democratic. But it may also be the case that a less "majoritarian" system will be one that gives greater weight to the interests of powerful minorities (or what we call "elites" when we disapprove of them.)

Future events in Cairo, where yesterday's rioters are celebrating a military coup against a democratically-elected government as if it were a popular revolution, will indicate which interpretation is closer to the truth.

**

Or maybe not. Cairo is not Brussels, nor Budapest, nor Lisbon. Still, as the erupting Portuguese political crisis over "Austerity" and the euro illustrates, and as our four articles on the European Union and the nationality principle discuss with rare scrupulousness, Europe is not without its own "problematic" attitudes to democracy. These arise from the uneasy cohabitation of the European Union with its own nation states.

With a few lagging exceptions, most European countries have largely solved their own internal difficulties with nationalism. They have domesticated it in two vital senses: first, every legal citizen is now, without dispute, a full member of the nation; second, by being largely satisfied, the nationalist passions have quieted down into a mild beneficent patriotism.

And if nationalism and democracy were once in conflict – see Ambrus Miskolczy's review of Lucian Boia's *Traps of History* for ironic and tragic examples of this in pre-war Romania – that is no longer so. National sovereignty in Europe is now democratic sovereignty. And as Roger Scruton demonstrates in his important essay, originally delivered to the Hungarian Academy of Letters and Sciences, a sober patriotism is an indispensable assistance to peoples and governments seeking to solve great economic and social problems by democratic means.

This desirable outcome is now threatened, as so often in history, by another desirable outcome: namely, the movement of European countries towards "ever-closer union". As two of Dr Scruton's friendly antagonists (Géza Jeszenszky and Péter Ákos Bod) rightly contend, the European Union has brought great benefits to ordinary Europeans in the forms of greater prosperity and economic opportunity. But integration has proceeded erratically, in the wrong order (a currency union before political integration), and far ahead of popular sentiment in most member states. The result is Europe's famous "democratic deficit".

That deficit was tolerable as long as nothing else important depended on it. But a democracy-lite EU is now insisting that its democratic members pursue "austerity" policies that the voters bitterly dislike. The latest result is Portugal's political crisis as fewer and fewer local politicians are prepared to accept political oblivion in defence of policies chosen by a remote bureaucracy disguised as Angela Merkel. To point out that most of those same voters want to remain in the euro when that requires the austerity they oppose is merely to re-state the problem: which is that the euro, like the EU itself, cuts the democratic link between the voters and government policy.

This is not an insoluble problem, as Péter Ákos Bod points out. National sovereignty, democracy and EU membership can be reconciled by a "workable modus vivendi". That solution, however, would probably have to include assigning fewer powers to Brussels and more to national parliaments closer to the voters.

Not an insoluble problem, then, but a problem nonetheless.

The friendliest of Scruton's interlocutors, George Jonas, turns the usual indictment of nationalism against its prosecutors in Brussels and elsewhere. If they fear that the ordinary citizen's love of country is the first step to hyper-nationalism, fascism, or simple irrationalism, how would their own loyalties fare under cross-examination? After all, their patriotism is to a country that doesn't yet exist. As Orwell points out, this kind of "transferred nationalism" is usually more irrational and zealous than the ordinary common-or-garden kind.

Irrationalism was certainly a marked feature of the self-styled "scientific" political doctrines of the first half of the 20th century on both Left and Right. In his ground-breaking investigation into Stalin's anti-Semitic 'doctors' plot", Tibor Pethő underlines the absurd ideological acrobatics that state officials performed in order to comply with the orders of the Soviet dictator and his Hungarian accomplice Mátyás Rákosi.

Rákosi had originally ordered the head of the secret police (ÁVH), Gábor Péter, to prepare a series of show trials at the end of 1952. In mid-preparation, however, he changed his mind: "The ÁVH leader was arrested on 3 January 1953 in Rákosi's villa on Lóránt Street. Péter arrived shortly before from Szuhakálló, the site of a mine disaster where he personally tried to identify the 'plotters' and 'diversionists'. (Even in the case of accidents, a culprit had to be found...)"

You couldn't make it up, as the British say.

But among those who could certainly make it up were the Romanian intellectuals who flirted with the extreme nationalism of the Legion of the Archangel Michael before the Second World War and with communism after it, sometimes consummating both relationships in succession with orgiastic cries, sometimes retreating into a guilty silence. With intellectual brilliance and an utter lack of commonsense, they adopted and preached one silly ideological novelty after another.

They are treated with dry-eyed irony by both Lucian Boia, author of *Traps of History,* and by our reviewer, Ambrus Miskolczy, and suffer appropriate fates at their hands. Thus, one intellectual ornament of the Legion, who was probably also working for the Germans, died suddenly of poisoning, "conforming with legionary tradition".

Sadly, Magda Lupescu, the flame-haired temptress and conspirator who became the King's mistress and famously arrived into Brazilian exile with almost seven hundred pieces of luggage, does not make an appearance in the dock. But she is suitably memorialised elsewhere in a limerick:

"I was stranded," said Madam Lupescu,
"When Royalty came to the rescue.
Now it's diamonds and pearls.
So, honestly, girls,
Is democracy better? I ask you."

Now, there's a girl who could have taught the average Romanian Nobel Prize winner a thing or two.

4 July 2013, Budapest

ENCOUNTERS WITH THE THIRD KIND: TURKEY'S NEW POLITICAL FORCES ARE MET BY OLD POLITICS

İlter Turan

EMERGENCE OF THE THIRD KIND

Few observers, if any, would have predicted that demonstrations that commenced at the Gezi Promenade of Taksim Square at the end of May over plans to build a shopping mall in the area would continue to capture the attention of both domestic and international audiences today. They are presenting a challenge to the government of Recep Tayyip Erdoğan, whose appearance of invincibility has been considerably tarnished. At the time of writing, protestors were continuing to stage stand-ins under the watchful eyes of frustrated but somewhat relaxed police officers.

Turkish authorities are used to demonstrations by students, labour unions, and others, which they quell with clubs and tear gas. As recently as 1 May, the governor of Istanbul had forbidden unions to celebrate May Day in Taksim Square, preventing those who insisted anyway by using sticks and volatile chemicals. Such "routine" events hardly capture global attention; life returns to normal in a day. It is possible that this time, the government thought that it could also easily terminate this protest with the usual harsh measures. To its surprise, the police encountered not only strong but mainly passive resistance. The numbers rushing to support the initial adventurers grew rapidly rather than declined.

What was different this time? Polls conducted among those who rallied on the Square show that a large majority had not participated in a political rally before and that only a small minority belonged to a political party. Many participants are students or well-educated young professionals. Such a mix of backgrounds is atypical in Turkey's confrontation-driven street politics that have usually been the domain of radical non-democratic organisations of the far right and left. Why has this unusual group taken to the streets?

Interviews with those participating at the demonstrations in Istanbul and sympathy rallies in other cities bring out two major complaints: the failure of government to consult the citizens in projects that affect their daily lives, and the implementation of a number of steps that are judged to intrude into the private lives of citizens.

The first point concerns differing understandings of democracy between the Prime Minister and the protestors. Erdoğan perceives democracy as receiving a mandate to rule the country for four years as he sees fit through elections, sometimes known as the "trustee" orientation. The protestors, on the other hand, conceptualise democracy as an ongoing process of mutual consultation between the occupants of elective office and the citizens. It is interesting that the protestors were neither partisan nor did they demand the resignation of the Prime Minister. They wanted to be listened to. Their only concrete demand was that the decision to reconstruct a military barracks on what is now a promenade be suspended to protect a rare green space in the city centre.

The second point relates to the proper scope of political intervention. In recent times, enacted legislation and speeches of the Prime Minister have delved into areas of life that the demonstrators felt were matters of individual choice. These encroachments have included such things as new restrictions on the sale of alcohol, the Prime Minister's pronouncement that anyone who imbibes is an alcoholic, his insistence that all married couples have three children, and the expansion of religion courses in primary and secondary education curricula. Looking at these objections, one might get the impression that this is the old laicist-religious conservative cleavage that has characterised Turkish politics for the entire life of the republic. Yet this would be inaccurate. The demonstrators included some religious groups and many others who did not share the same political preferences. Their mutual respect for differences was epitomised on the occasion of Friday prayers where those not praying formed a circle around those who did, to insure that they could pray undisturbed. They also engaged in the unheard of exercise of cleaning the garbage from the areas where they had demonstrated the day before.

It seems that these developments point to the emergence of a new political animal, a third kind so to speak, in Turkish politics: the socially engaged individual citizen who expects a government to be open to regular communication with citizens, more responsive to citizen preferences, and more respectful of the individual's privacy. Expressed differently they want more refined democratic governance: limited not interventionist, pluralistic not monistic, inclusionary not exclusionary. Does the government, especially the Prime Minister, see it this way too?

NEW POLITICS, OLD TIME RESPONSES

When protests started, the government initially seemed confused. Neither the crowd nor its manner of behaviour looked familiar. It did not take the authorities long, however, to decide that challenging the authority of the government could not be ignored in a country where "rule of law" prevailed. Crowds were gassed and clubbed and tents some had set up in the promenade were burned. Istanbul's governor explained that the protest movement was led by suspicious elements who were well known to the authorities, and good citizens should stay home. To the surprise of the authorities, however, the crowds returned in larger numbers. Furthermore, many citizens appeared to feel that disproportionate force had been used to drive the demonstrators off Taksim Square, and "public enemy" explanations were found not to be particularly persuasive.

During the next two weeks, what had now become a crisis was managed under the leadership of the Prime Minister, who pursued a two-pronged strategy of simultaneously communicating with the protestors and discrediting them. In implementing the first part, Erdoğan refrained from using coercive instruments of the state to vacate the Square and similar places in other cities, saying that protestors should leave voluntarily. He seemed open to hearing the demands of protesters, holding long chats with some prominent demonstrators. He announced that the barracks would be built but as a city museum; and conceded that he would await the administrative court decision regarding zoning changes and building permits before implementing the project. After these gestures and reminding all that he did not have unlimited patience (i.e. that the option of using force was never away), he asked that everyone clear the Square. After allowing little time for vacating the area, the police moved in and cleared it through well established methods.

In carrying out the second part of his strategy, he developed a set of arguments intended to discredit the protests and protestors, a path that was typical of old politics. In essence, it promoted political polarisation between his supporters and those sympathising with the protestors, whom he tried to associate with the opposition. To begin with, Erdoğan argued that there was a conspiracy to stop Turkey's enviable economic and political ascent in the international arena. It seems that although many internal and external actors were involved in it, it was the "interest lobby", meaning actors who benefit from having the interest rates remain high, that led the list. Other actors, whose identity could only be inferred, seemed to include many of Turkey's friends and allies. The Prime Minister insinuated that conspirators also included mainly Istanbul-based old industrial conglomerates that have shied away from an expressly pro-government orientation. One could not be too careful, he said, about these ill-intentioned elements.

External threat arguments were complemented by disinformation about the protestors. It was rumoured, for example, that those who had taken refuge in a mosque down the hill from Taksim Square had consumed alcoholic beverages and engaged in sex on the premises, an accusation that the Imam of the facility immediately denied. Similarly, it was said that a conservatively dressed young lady with a baby had been attacked, beaten and rendered unconscious by 100 bare-bodied men wearing leather gloves who had then proceeded to urinate on her. Observers have condemned the incident but have expressed surprise that in a city where almost every public arena is surveyed by cameras, none of these 100 men have been seen by other witnesses, identified, or caught.

The protests have also been attributed to the doings of the major opposition party. The Prime Minister recalled the Republican People's Party's rule as years of do-nothing administrations that exposed people to undeserved deprivations and said the party was jealous of the success of his government and was trying to block further progress to an even more prosperous Turkey.

Finally, to show that he continued to enjoy the support of the masses, Erdoğan organised big rallies in major towns, starting with Ankara and Istanbul and then moving to conservative centres in Central and Eastern Turkey, popularising some of the themes above.

The government's reaction to the challenge facing it is reminiscent of the efforts of the right wing Nationalist Front Coalitions of 1973–80, who tried to tighten their ranks by pursuing polarisation policies in the face of strong opposition. In this way, they hoped to reinforce the commitment of the supporters to their current parties and the status quo, and they seem to have achieved this at least in the short term.

The Turkish government is encountering a challenge from forces that its own economic success strengthened during the last ten years. Its responses to what amounts to a demand for a more refined democracy have so far been met with not so well-refined responses. But some questions still need to be asked and answered: Have the recent events produced irreversible changes in Turkish politics? Will the government be able to reconstitute the status quo? What will the effects of these changes in Turkey's domestic and external relations be? The future of Turkish politics depends on the answers to these questions, which remain to be seen.

We acknowledge the kind co-operation of the German Marshall Foundation of the United States in our publication of this article.

THE NEED FOR NATIONS

Roger Scruton

The project of European integration, advanced by politicians and elites of defeated nations in the wake of the Second World War, was founded on the belief that nationhood and national self-determination were the prime causes of the wars that had ruined Europe. There were disputes as to who started it: Napoleon? Bismarck? The French Revolutionaries? The Revolutionaries of 1848? The Reactionaries and Monarchists? Metternich? Talleyrand? Garibaldi? Fichte? Wagner? Louis XIV? But, however far back you went, in the eyes of the post-war political survivors, you came across the demon of nationalism, locked in conflict with the pure spirit of Enlightenment. As a result of this founding myth European integration was conceived in one-dimensional terms, as a process of ever-increasing *unity,* under a centralised structure of command. Each increase in central power was to be matched by a diminution of national power.

In other words, the political process in Europe was to be endowed with a *direction.* It is not a direction that the people of Europe have chosen, and every time they are given the chance to vote they reject it – hence everything is done to ensure that they never have the chance to vote. The process moves always towards centralisation, top-down control, dictatorship by unelected bureaucrats and judges, cancellation of laws passed by elected parliaments, constitutional treaties framed without any input whatsoever from the people. In the current debt crisis the European elite – composed largely of the governing circles in France and Germany – has assumed the right to depose the elected governments of Greece and Italy, and to impose their own henchmen, chosen from the ranks of obedient apparatchiks. Meanwhile Hungary is constantly assailed with provocative questions and threats of investigation, for having dared to pass its own laws about matters in which the European political class has tacitly assumed sovereignty. In this way, the process is moving always towards imperial government, making very clear that the opposite of nationhood is not Enlightenment but Empire. And only one thing stands opposed to this result, and that is the national sentiments of the European people.

As an Englishman and a lover of the civilisation of Rome I am not opposed to Empire. But it is important to recognise what it involves and to distinguish the good from the bad forms of it. In my view the good forms serve to protect local loyalties and customs under a canopy of civilisation and law; the bad forms try to extinguish local customs and rival loyalties and to replace them by a lawless and centralised power. The European Union has elements of both arrangements: but it suffers from one overwhelming defect, which is that it has never persuaded the people of Europe to accept it. Europe is, and in my view has ever been, a civilisation of nation states, founded on a specific kind of pre-political allegiance, which is the allegiance that puts territory and custom first and religion and dynasty second in the order of government. Give them a voice, therefore, and the people of Europe will express their loyalties in those terms. In so far as they have *unconditional* loyalties — loyalties that are a matter of identity rather than agreement — they take a national form.

The political class in Europe does not like this, and as a result has demonised the direct expression of national sentiments. Speak up for Jeanne d'Arc and *le pays réel*, for the "sceptred isle" and St George, for Lemmenkäinen's gloomy forests and the "true Finns" who roam in them, and you will be called a fascist, a racist and an extremist. There is a liturgy of denunciation here that is repeated all across Europe by a political class that affects to despise ordinary loyalties while surreptitiously depending on them. In recent years Hungary has been a particular target of attack. There are extraneous reasons for it in Hungarian history, of course, and I do not need to remind you of them. But those reasons are not what animate the European elite. The present Hungarian government, by making issues of national identity and national sentiment fundamental to its platform, has excited a strong and censorious response from the European Union, regardless of any other grounds for such disapproval.

On the other hand, national sentiment is, for most ordinary Europeans, the only publicly available and publicly shared motive that will justify sacrifice in the common cause — the only source of obligation in the public sphere that is not a matter of what can be bought and sold. In so far as people do not vote to line their own pockets, it is because they also vote to protect a shared identity from the predations of those who do not belong to it, and who are attempting to pillage an inheritance to which they are not entitled. Philip Bobbitt has argued that one major effect of the wars between nation states in Europe has been the replacement of the nation state with the "market state" — the state conceived as a firm, offering benefits in exchange for duties, which we are free to join or to leave as we choose. (See *The Shield of Achilles*.) If this were true, then the nation, as an identity-forming community, would have lost its leading role in defining political choices and loyalties. Indeed, we would have emerged from the world of political loyalty altogether, into a realm of self-interested negotiations, in which sacrifices are no longer accepted, and perhaps no longer required. But if the present crisis has convinced us of nothing else, it has surely brought home to us that the capacity for sacrifice is the pre-condition of enduring communities, and that when the chips are down politicians both demand sacrifice and expect to receive it.

We have been made well aware by the Islamists that not everyone accepts the nation as the fount of unconditional loyalty. The followers of Sayyid Qutb, the leader of Egypt's Muslim Brotherhood in the 1950s and 1960s, tell us that national obedience is a form of idolatry, and that it is to Allah alone that obedience is owed. There is a direct connection between those ideas and the failure of Middle Eastern countries to acquire stability since the fall of the Ottoman Empire and their division into nation states. The European nations have never whole-heartedly accepted that kind of theocratic absolutism, and firmly rejected it at the Treaty of Westphalia. The problem for Europe is that the ensuing centuries of territorial jurisdiction have implanted sentiments that do not fit easily into any kind of imperial ambition. In the circumstances of modern democratic government it is only on behalf of the nation that people are prepared to think outside the frame of self-interest. Hence the new imperial project has entered into conflict with the only source of sentiment upon which it could conceivably draw for its legitimacy. The nation states are not equally stable, equally democratic, equally free or equally obedient to the rule of law. But they alone inspire the obedience of the European people, and without them there is no way that the machinery of the Union can act. By replacing national accountability with distant bureaucracy, that machinery has left people disarmed and bewildered in the face of the current crisis.

We see this clearly in the matter of the common currency. The euro, imposed without proof that the people of the "Eurozone" had any desire for it, was immediately understood, by many politicians in the Mediterranean, as a way of enlarging the national debt. This was very obviously the case in Greece. Bonds issued in euros would benefit from the strength and probity of the Northern economies, and would be regarded as safe bets by investors who would not dream of buying bonds issued in drachmas. And the people of Greece agreed, since nobody alerted them to the cost – the *national* cost – that will be paid, once the Eurozone breaks up, as surely it must. Now that the day of reckoning is approaching, people all across the continent sense the need to prepare themselves for hard times. In a crisis people "take stock", which means that they retreat to the primary source of their social attachment, and prepare to defend it. They do not do this consciously. But they do it nevertheless, and the futile attempt by the politicians to denounce the "extremism" of the people whose inheritance they have squandered merely exacerbates the reaction. But the situation is not a happy one, since there is no trans-national idea of Europe to which the politician can appeal by way of identifying an object of loyalty outside the borders of the nation state. The half-century of peace and prosperity has fed upon the European cultural inheritance without renewing it. For it is all but impossible for a European politician to evoke the civilisation of Europe when its source – the Christian religion – has been expunged from official documents and openly repudiated by the European courts. One ground of the current attacks on the "nationalist" government of Hungary by the European Commission is that the Hungarians have drawn up a constitution which, in its preamble, describes the Hungarians as a "Christian nation": two words that have been expunged from the official vocabulary of Europe. Indeed, if you look at the verdicts of the European courts, and especially of the Court of Human Rights, you will find a systematic bias against Christianity and Christians which has no other explanation than the ideological assumptions on which the European project has been built.

The constitutional treaties likewise have made a point of granting no favours to the Christian faith or to the morality that has sprung from it. A "cult of the minority" has been imposed from above, as a kind of rebuke to the people of Europe for being Europeans in spirit. This official multiculturalism has done nothing to reconcile immigrant communities to their new surroundings; instead it has destroyed much that was confident and joyful in the national cultures of Europe and rejected the Christian pieties in favour of a kind of morose materialism.

The result of official multiculturalism is in fact cultural blindness – an inability to perceive the real cultural distinctions that obtain across the European continent and which are rooted in the custom and history of the nation states. If the architects of the euro had taken national cultures properly into account they would have known that the effect of imposing a single currency on Greece and Germany would be to encourage Greece to transfer its debts to Germany, on the understanding that the further away the creditor the less the obligation to repay. They would have recognised that laws, obligations and sovereignty do not have quite the same meaning in the Mediterranean as they do on the Baltic, and that in a society used to kleptocratic government the fairest way out of an economic crisis is by devaluation – in other words, by stealing equally from everybody. And they would have recognised that, by imposing a single currency on Greece and Germany nevertheless, they would sow the seeds of mutual resentment.

Why did the architects of the euro not know those things? The answer is to be found deep within the European project. Cultural facts were simply *unperceivable* to the Eurocrats. Allowing themselves to perceive culture would be tantamount to recognising that their project was an impossible one. This would have mattered less if they had another project with which to replace it. But – like all radical projects, communism being the archetype – that of the European Union was conceived without a Plan B. Hence it is destined to collapse and, in the course of its collapse, to drag our continent down. An enormous pool of pretence has accumulated at the centre of the project, while the political class skirmishes at the edges, in an attempt to fend off the constant assaults of reality.

Thus we have to pretend that the long-observed distinctions between the Protestant North of our continent and the Catholic and Orthodox South is of no economic significance. Being a cultural fact it is unperceivable, notwithstanding Weber's (admittedly exaggerated) attempt to make it central to economic history. The difference between the culture of common law and that of the *code Napoléon* has likewise been ignored, at the cost of alienating the British and the Danes, for whom law has ever been a social rather than a political product. The distinction between the Roman and the Ottoman legal legacies has been set aside, as has that between countries where law is certain and judges incorruptible and places where law is only the last resort in a system of bribes. Times and speeds of work, and the balance between work and leisure, which go to the heart of every community since they define its relation to time, are ignored, or else regimented by a futile edict from the centre. All that is distinctive of the Hungarian experience – the shock of the Treaty of Trianon, which divided the Hungarian people from one another, the distinctive culture of a land-locked country in which a large population of Roma has never properly settled, the still present record of the country's struggle against Islamic domination – all this too has been ignored. And everything is to be brought into line by those frightening courts – the European Court of Justice and the European Court of Human Rights – whose unelected judges never pay the cost of their decisions, and whose agenda of "non-discrimination" and "ever-closer union" is calculated to wipe away the traces of local loyalties, family-based morality and rooted ways of life. Not surprisingly, when you build an empire on such massive pretences, it very soon becomes unstable.

We can rescue Europe, it seems to me, only if we can recover the project that Charles de Gaulle wished to place at its heart, and which was effectively scotched by Jean Monnet – the project of a Europe of Nations. It will not be easy to unravel the web of regulations and edicts contained in the 180,000 pages of the *acquis communautaire*; nor will it be easy to redefine the roles and the structures of the European courts and the competences of the European Institutions. But the most difficult thing will be to obtain agreement on what national sovereignty really means. In particular, what will sovereignty mean in the aftermath of the European Union? Conservative politicians in Britain often speak of recapturing powers from Brussels, as though these powers would not have been altered by captivity, and as though they could be easily domesticated when they are brought back home. This is like Menelaus thinking that home life in Mycenae would be just the same when he had returned victorious from Troy, the recaptured Helen obediently trotting behind, as it was in the good old days before she left.

The situation of Europe today reminds us that by conceiving pre-political loyalties in national, rather than religious terms, European civilisation has made room for the Enlightenment. The national idea is not the enemy of Enlightenment but its necessary precondition. National loyalty marginalises loyalties of family, tribe and faith, and places before the citizen's eyes, as the focus of his patriotic feeling, not a person or a group but a country. This country is defined by a territory, and by the history, culture and law that have made that territory *ours*. It is the emergence of territory from behind religion, tribe and dynasty that characterises the nationalist art and literature of the 19th century, and the national anthems of the self-identifying nations were conceived as invocations of home, in the manner of Sibelius's *Finlandia* or the unofficial national anthem of England, "Land of Hope and Glory".

In short, Enlightenment means borders. Take away borders, and people begin to identify themselves not by territory and law, but by tribe, race or religion. Nationality is composed of land, together with the narrative of its possession. It is this form of territorial loyalty that has enabled people in Western democracies to exist side by side, respecting each other's rights as citizens, despite radical differences in faith, and without any bonds of family, kinship or long-term local custom to sustain the solidarity between them. For on the foundation of territorial attachment it has been possible to build a kind of civic patriotism, which acknowledges institutions and laws as shared possessions, and which can extend a welcome to those who have entered the social contract from outside. You cannot immigrate into a tribe, a family or a faith; but you can immigrate into a country, provided you are prepared to obey the rules that make that country into a home.

National loyalty is not known everywhere in the world. Consider Somalia. People sometimes refer to Somalia as a "failed state", since it has no central government capable of making decisions on behalf of the people as a whole, or of imposing any kind of legal order. But the real trouble with Somalia is that it is a failed nation. It has never developed the kind of secular, territorial and law-minded sovereignty that makes it possible for a country to shape itself as a nation state rather than an assemblage of competing tribes and families.

The same is true of many other countries in which Islam is the dominant faith. Even if such countries do function as states, like Pakistan, they are often failures as nations. They seem not to generate the kind of territorial loyalty that would enable people of different faiths, different kinship networks, different tribes to live peacefully side by side, and also to fight side by side on behalf of their common homeland. They are more likely to fight each other for possession of the homeland than to join forces in protecting it. And their recent history might lead us to wonder whether there is not, in the end, a deep conflict between Islamic conceptions of community and the conceptions that have fed our own idea of national sovereignty. Maybe the nation state is an anti-Islamic idea. Certainly that is what Sayyid Qutb would have us believe. Living in "the shade of the Koran", as he famously put it, you surrender to God, not to mortals. And all lesser jurisdictions, including those founded on territory, custom and man-made law, are abolished by the supreme jurisdiction of the Almighty. (*Fi zilâl al-qur'ân*.) Ayatollah Khomeini said the same, when he dismissed patriotism as paganism.

This observation is, of course, pertinent to the Middle East today, where we find the remnants of a great Islamic Empire divided into nation states. With a few exceptions this division is the result of boundaries drawn on the map by Western powers, and notably by Britain and France as a result of the Sykes–Picot accords of 1917. It is hardly surprising if Iraq, for example, has had such a chequered history as a nation state, given that it has been only spasmodically a state, and never a nation. It may be that Kurds, Sunnite Arabs and Shi'ites in Iraq could all come, in time, to see themselves as Iraqis. But this identity will be fragile and fissiparous, and in any conflict the three groups will identify themselves in opposition to each other. Indeed, it is only the Kurds who seem to have a developed *national* identity, and it is an identity opposed to that of the state in which they are included. As for the Shi'ites, their primary loyalty is religious, and they look to the homeland of Shi'ism in Iran as a model in turbulent times. Today we are witnessing the collapse of civil order in Syria, a country which has never been a nation state, but in which one minority sect, the 'Alawites, controlled the main centres of power, striving for legitimacy through aggressive territorial claims against Lebanon and Israel. The current civil war is degenerating into a war between the sects, with Christians as the principal victims.

The vexed question of Islam and modernity takes us too far from our topic; suffice it to say that tribe and creed have always been more important than sovereignty in Islamic ways of thinking, and the non-emergence of nations in the Middle East is partly explained by this, as is their embryonic emergence in those countries, like Lebanon and Egypt, with substantial Christian minorities, maintaining long-standing trade links with Europe.

More importantly, I have no doubt that it is the long centuries of Christian dominance in Europe which laid the foundations of national loyalty, as a loyalty above those of faith and family, and on which a secular jurisdiction and an order of citizenship can be founded. It may sound paradoxical to identify a religion as the major force behind the development of secular government. But we should remember the peculiar circumstances in which Christianity entered the world. The Jews were a closed community, bound in a tight web of religious legalisms, but governed from Rome by a law which made no reference to any God and which offered an ideal of citizenship to which every free subject of the Empire might aspire.

Christ found himself in conflict with the legalism of his fellow Jews, and in broad sympathy with the idea of secular government – hence his famous words in the parable of the Tribute Money: render unto Caesar what is Caesar's and to God what is God's. The Christian faith was shaped by St Paul for the use of communities within the Empire, who wanted only space to pursue their worship, and had no intention of challenging the secular powers. Hence "the powers that be are ordained of God" (Romans 13). And this idea of dual loyalty continued after Constantine, being endorsed by Pope Gelasius the First in the 6th century, in his doctrine of the two swords given to mankind for their government, that which guards the body politic, and that which guards the individual soul. It is this deep endorsement of secular law by the early Church that was responsible for the subsequent developments in Europe – through the Reformation and the Enlightenment – to the purely territorial law that prevails in the West today.

It is very clear from the history of our continent, that new forms of solidarity have here come into being which owe much to the Christian inheritance, but which are premised on the assumption that legitimacy is a man-made and not a God-bestowed achievement. Nations emerged as forms of pre-political order that contain within themselves the principles that would legitimise sovereign government. Political theorists of the Enlightenment such as Locke and Rousseau tried to encapsulate this legitimising process in a social contract, by which the members of society form an agreement to be governed in a certain way in exchange for renouncing the state of nature. But it is surely obvious that if people assemble to consider a contract that will unite them, it is because they already belong together, already acknowledge that the welfare of each depends upon the actions of all. A contract, however strong its terms, can never establish more than a *conditional* obligation, whereas political order depends, in the end, on an unconditional component, as do marriage and the family. Without this unconditional component no community can survive a real crisis.

The social contract therefore establishes a form of government that will protect and perpetuate an allegiance that precedes the contract and makes it possible. This allegiance is shaped by history and territory, and by all the forms of association that spring from these, notably language, customary law and religious observance. Seeing things in this way, religious observance is demoted to one factor among others, and is reshaped as a *subject* of law, rather than a source of it. That, to my mind, is the great achievement of European civilisation: to have placed man-made law at the heart of the community, to have subordinated all associations, including those stemming from religion, to the demands of the secular jurisdiction, and to have established the institutions through which law can adapt to changes in social life instead of blurting out some "eternal" message revealed in circumstances that have vanished, leaving no other trace.

However, law so conceived is territorial and therefore national. It is a law that defines boundaries, beyond which its writ does not run. Claims to jurisdiction from a place outside those boundaries are fiercely resisted, as we know from the history of England and from the conflict between the crown and the papacy that has been decisive in forming many of the nation states of Europe. When it is proposed that the *corpus iuris* should permit European courts to charge British citizens with criminal offences, and extradite them to the place most convenient for their trial, it is hardly surprising that British people receive this suggestion with outrage. Their conception of law is the common law conception, which does not permit people to be held indefinitely without trial, and which depends for its authority on the "law of the land", as embodied in cases decided in the sovereign territory of the English Crown. This attachment of law to territory is not some arbitrary limitation, as though there were a universal jurisdiction from which local jurisdictions are derived by restriction. It is the very essence of law, as the European experience has defined it. We are heirs to a conception of law as arising from the attempt to settle conflicts, to establish institutions, to adjudicate rights and duties, among people who are bound to each other as neighbours. Law, as we know it, is produced by the place that needed it, and is marked by the history of that place. (The contrast with the *Shari'ah* is obvious, as is the contrast with the "natural law" of the stoics and the Universal Church.)

Hence the attempt to build a European Empire of laws that depend upon no national allegiance for their authority is not merely bound to fail. It is likely also to undermine the authority of secular law in the minds of the European people. There is already in the social contract theories of the eighteenth century a kind of wishful thinking about human nature, a belief that people can reshape all their obligations without reference to their affections, so as to produce an abstract calculus of rights and duties in the place of their contingent and historical ties. The French Revolutionaries began their seizure of power in this way, proposing a declaration of the rights of man and the citizen that would sweep away all the arbitrary arrangements of history and place Reason on the throne that had previously been occupied by a mere human being, who had arrived there by the accident of succession. But within weeks of the Declaration the country was being governed in the name of the Nation, the *Patrie*, and the old contingent association was being summoned in another and (to my mind) far more dangerous form, in order to fill the gap in people's affections that had been made by the destruction of customary loyalty, religious usage and the unquestioned ways of neighbourhood. This was clearly perceived by Burke, who reminded his readers that human beings are thrown together by accidents that they do not choose, and derive their affections not from their decisions but from their circumstances. It is proximity, not reason, that is the foundation of ordinary charitable feeling. Take that thought seriously, and you quickly come to see that territorial forms of association are the best remedy that we have against the divisive call of ideology. National attachment is precisely what prevents "extremism" from taking hold of the ordinary conscience.

This is why we must distinguish national loyalty, which is the sine qua non of consensual government in the modern world, from nationalism, which is a belligerent ideology that looks for a source of government higher than the routines of settlement and neighbourhood. Nationalism is an ideological attempt to *supplant* customary and neighbourly loyalties with something more like a religious loyalty – a loyalty based on doctrine and commitment. Ordinary national loyalty, by contrast, is the by-product of settlement. It comes about because people have ways of resolving their disputes, ways of getting together, ways of cooperating, ways of celebrating and worshipping that seal the bond between them without ever making that bond explicit as a doctrine. This is surely how ordinary people live, and it is at the root of all that is best in human society, namely that we are attached to what goes on around us, grow together with it, and learn the ways of peaceful association as *our* ways, which are right because they are ours and because they unite us with those who came before us and those for whom we will in turn make way. Seen in that way national feelings are not just natural, they are essentially *legitimising*. They call upon the sources of social affection, and bestow that affection on customs that have proved their worth over time, by enabling a community to settle its disputes and achieve equilibrium in the changing circumstances of life.

National sentiments enable people successfully to defend themselves in wartime. But they are also essential in peacetime too. This we are now seeing in Europe, as the sovereign debt crisis begins to affect the lives of ordinary people. Governments are calling on their citizens to make sacrifices for the common good. They are not asking them to make sacrifices for "Europe", still less for the European Union. If they were to use this language then they would be forced to recognise that Europe is not the bureaucratic machine that has conferred upon them the small measure of legitimacy that they can claim, but a spiritual inheritance that the machine has tried to extirpate. Hence the only invocations that they can make address national sentiments. They speak of the need to pull together, for the sake of *our* community, and at every point their language invokes the contingencies of human affection, that make it possible for people to give up something for the sake of others – a habit of mind that social democracies do not normally encourage. They are not speaking the language of nationalism, but the language of attachment, which is something entirely different. Their response to the crisis of Europe reveals that the nation state is not the problem but the solution – it contains within itself the only motives to which politicians can now appeal, when the effects of the European project are finally being felt across the continent.

In conclusion I must say something about the situation of Hungary today, as I understand it, and the relevance of the national idea to the Hungarians. That Hungary is a special case is evident. The Hungarian language is an isolated remnant of a linguistic group that was for the most part extinguished by the Indo-European migrations, and bares little or no relation to any of the surrounding tongues. Ordinary uneducated Hungarians are therefore isolated from their immediate neighbours by their language. They have also been isolated from one another by the forcible division of their territory at the end of the First World War. The remnant of territory that they still enjoy is shared with a substantial minority of Roma, whose unsettled ways are often resented by their neighbours, but whose cause inevitably gathers support in the wider world. The Jewish minority that survived the Nazi occupation suffered further persecution under the communists, but nevertheless is active in making its presence known. Many of the Budapest intelligentsia are Jewish, and form part of the extensive networks around the Soros Empire. People in these networks include many who are rightly suspicious of nationalism, regard nationalism as the major cause of the tragedy of Central Europe in the 20th century, and do not distinguish nationalism from the kind of national loyalty that I have defended in this talk. Moreover, as the world knows, indigenous anti-Semitism still plays a part in Hungarian society and politics, and presents an obstacle to the emergence of a shared national loyalty among ethnic Hungarians and Jews.

Those are only some of the factors that stand in the way of a collective pre-political attachment in this part of the world. The European Union offers an idea of citizenship which is in fact a citizenship of nowhere. It encourages people to move from their homeland and to settle elsewhere in the Union, and inevitably those who move are the educated class, whose departure deprives the country of its teachers, doctors, lawyers and surgeons, and provides no replacements for them. The EU also encourages the sale of land to foreign nationals – so building a non-resident landlord class, which has no personal interest in the beauty and moral order of rural life, and which sees land merely as an investment, to be put to use. This has led, and will lead, to tensions of a kind that can be resolved only by a firm political will.

For there is no alternative to nationality. If the government in Budapest is to enjoy legitimacy, that legitimacy must come from below, from the people whose unity and identity are expressed in the workings of government. This legitimacy must be inherited by each government, whether right or left, whether minority or majority. It must not be a loyalty of cliques, or a reprimand to the peasantry issued by the intellectuals of Budapest, or an edict issued by the true Hungarians in the villages against the traitors in the city. The electorate itself must be identified in territorial terms, since the jurisdiction is territorial, not ethnic or religious. The alternative is fragmentation, as competing ethnic groups or factional interests form parties whose purpose is not to rule in the interest of everyone, but to pillage for the sake of the group. I do not wish to comment here on the existing political parties in Hungary or to raise the question whether any of them has seen government as an opportunity for plunder rather than a duty to secure the common good. But I do know that, until the institutions of government are seen by Hungarians as representing the country, rather than some faction within it, the government will suffer a deficit of legitimacy. It will then lose its principal advantage over the EU in its battle for the affections of the Hungarian people.

This is a written version of the lecture that Roger Scruton gave at the Hungarian Academy of Sciences. We acknowledge the kindness of Mr Scruton in giving us this essay for publication in English.

A MODERATE NATIONALIST MAY BE
THE SOLUTION

George Jonas

When the World Jewish Congress opened its 14th plenary session in Budapest last month, its choice of the Hungarian capital for the three-day event went beyond the amenities and attractions offered by the historic city. In the past three years Hungary has become a key battleground for Europe's soul.

What's going on in Hungary – or, for that matter, in Europe? This is hard to address without first addressing what went on in Hungary and Europe before. The trouble is, addressing it might make readers miss a few meals. Worse, it may take them into the impenetrable thicket of root causes.

Using root causes as apologies for the deeds of nations (or the misdeeds of governments) has given root causes a bad name. When identified, they rarely explain much and usually excuse nothing. Telling people more than they want to know is unwise. Readers curious why Brussels is having kittens if Budapest amends Hungary's constitution aren't necessarily bucking for a graduate degree in European history.

Knowing history may not be so helpful anyway. With apologies to George Santayana, remembering *no* history may be better than remembering too much and drawing the wrong conclusions from it. People are condemned to repeat history less often for their failure to recall it than for recalling it too well – or, even worse, too insistently.

The Soviet Union's collapse, taken for granted these days, was a world-shaking event twenty-one years ago. The implosion, sudden as it seemed in its unexpectedness, in fact played out over a period of two nail-biting years. Between the fall of 1989, when the Berlin Wall came crashing down and Hungary permitted thousands of East German defector "tourists" to use its soil to escape to the West, and 31 December 1991, when the Soviet hammer-and-sickle was lowered for the last time from the flagpole of the Kremlin, the stricken red giant could have tried to reassert itself. Many observers took it for granted that it would, but – except for the feeble "August Putsch" of 1991, that saw reform-communist leader Mikhail Gorbachev put briefly under house arrest by "hard-line" communists of the old school, who lacked any capacity for a follow up – it never did.

The twenty years that followed were a different story. The communist functionaries and their circles that ruled the Red Empire didn't just vanish into thin air. The immense vacuum of power and ideology created by the sudden removal of the Marxist-Leninist model attracted various political forces, policy proposals, ideas and ambitions in the "Eastern bloc" or former Warsaw Pact countries.

From day one, contenders included streetwise survivors of the defunct communist regimes trying to sneak back into power. Unlike former Nazis after the defeat of Hitler, ex-communists were well positioned for a comeback. Red cadres, administrative or technological, did not have to face the equivalent of "de-Nazification". After some dislocation, often minimal, many managed to continue in key positions.

Proponents of a Nazi heritage still existed as communism collapsed: malicious ghosts that remained un-exorcised after the Second World War. Following the regime change, they remained – wisely – invisible at first. They would have found no echoes in the early 1990s, and they could sense it.

Nazism, short for national socialism, is a malignancy inside the body politic. In our time it has culminated in near-successful attempts at genocide. It is incurable, and killing it isn't enough: a stake must be driven through its heart. Some international-socialist admirers of the centrally directed state believe Nazism originates in nationalism, ethnic nationalism in particular, and if nationalism could be eliminated, Nazism would vanish with it. The European Union would in all likelihood endorse this proposition, partly because official Brussels would consider it to be true, and also because when viewed from its own eurocratic perspective, nationalism, especially ethnic nationalism, whether it leads to Nazism or not, is almost as undesirable.

Others, myself included, think this is nonsense. Far from inevitably leading to malignancies or evils, nationalism is an organising principle, one of many available to human communities, no more intrinsically harmful or dangerous than affection or loyalty of any other kind. Far from conjuring them up, affection and loyalty for one's country should block or filter out evil things.

An understandable inability to forget history was the WJC's reason on 5 May for choosing to congregate on the Pest side of the Danube, overlooking the bank where 68 years ago Hungarian Nazis had been summarily executing Hungarian

Jews they had run out of time to deport to Auschwitz. The delegates gathered there to discuss, as one wire service put it, "a rise in far-right extremism and anti-Semitism in Europe, including Hungary".

In this phrasing, the current battle for Europe's soul would seem like the battle for Europe's soil seventy years ago, but it isn't. The forces arrayed against each other today are nothing like a Western-style democratic centre battling a Nazi-style far right. Even a Soviet-style far left is gone. Today's antagonists resemble their predecessors only in that they, too, form temporary coalitions of past and future foes.

The battle lines for now are between the Knights of Eurocracy and the bewildered inhabitants of their realm, who went to bed one night as Danes, Greeks, Poles, Hungarians, Italians, etc., to wake up next morning as vassals of Brussels. Yes, they did want to join, but they thought Europe was a club. They did not know it was a religious order, and of a faith in which few if any believed.

The European Union's side includes a post-communist oligarchic crime syndicate (I'm describing Hungary's socialist government between 2002–2010 in terms no worse than its own leader did in a leaked speech to the party faithful) in bed with suitably multicultural, metrosexual and matriarchal devotees of a centrally planned social-democratic Eurocracy, complete with camp followers of militant pacifists, Internet-hacking techno-egalitarians and advance waves of minaret-building Islamist theocrats posturing around them, who have sold themselves to the world's media as a "progressive" democratic centre supposedly standing firm against a far-right tide sweeping Europe back unto the rocks of the 1930s. It is a tide, all right, but it's far-right only for those who view Woodrow Wilson (US president 1913–1921) as far-right. He favoured national self-determination. It is a tide the philosopher Roger Scruton calls "the national sentiments of the European people".

Some blame the rising of the tide on Hungary's Prime Minister, Viktor Orbán. Leader of a centre-right coalition between Fidesz, his own party of young (by now middle-aged) conservatives and Hungary's traditional Christian Democrats, Orbán has adamantly refused to throw out the baby of the nation state with the bathwater of anti-Semitism, chauvinism, irredentism and other hypertrophies of national identity. This put him on the wrong side of the progressive multiculturalist bureaucracies of the European Union who view most manifestations of nationalism with misgivings.

On 5 May, as he welcomed WJC's 500 uneasy delegates, Orbán put the question starkly:

"Ladies and gentlemen," he asked, "where did we go wrong in Europe during the past twenty years? We finally destroyed communism. We put an end to the Cold War. Europe was given the chance to once again be the continent of peace, cohabitation, understanding and tolerance. And here we are twenty years later and are searching for a cure for increasing intolerance and anti-Semitism. What happened to us?"

It seemed an honest question and the answer was equally straightforward: "We Hungarians think", Orbán said, "that it was a mistake to believe that a community with a weak national and religious identity would give us a better chance of peaceful cohabitation. Today, it seems that a strong identity provides better bedrock for mutual acknowledgement and respect."

Is Hungary's leader right or wrong? At home, Orbán has strong supporters and bitter opponents; abroad, he has bitter opponents. His earliest choice as Prime Minister, much reviled, was to update Hungary's constitution, once his sweeping electoral victory in 2010 made this choice legally available to him. His Hungary became more of a nation state and less of a caravanserai.

People who didn't like it questioned its legitimacy. I had reservations myself (I rather enjoy caravanserais) but its legitimacy seemed impeccable. Every constitution sets out ways in which it can be amended. Hungary's puts the almost impossible burden of a two-thirds parliamentary majority on a government that would make unilateral amendments. As it happened, Orbán's coalition achieved it in 2010. After eight years of being run into the ground by a succession of left-wing politicians of self-confessed corruption and incompetence, the voters returned Orbán to power with a majority that permitted him to go to town. He did. Wise? Maybe not. Legitimate? Yes.

Orbán rejected a world-view taken for granted by post-modern cultural relativists. He embraced national tradition and Christian virtues within a secular state. Wouldn't be my ideal, but then I didn't run for office in Budapest. He did.

Orbán's view of anti-Semitism is as dim as any post-modern progressive multiculturalist's, but he comes to it by a different route. He finds anti-Semitism abhorrent (a) because it is stupid; (b) because it goes against Hungary's traditions of chivalry and hospitality that made Jews settle there in the first place; and (c) because anti-Semitism contradicts basic Christian values.

The elite who set the tone of Europe's progressive, social democratic multicultural societies, view such reasons for not being an anti-Semite as bad as being one, if not worse. They point out that all these splendid national traditions and Christian virtues existed three-quarters of a century ago, yet did nothing to prevent the brutal extermination of millions of men, women and children in Nazi-occupied Europe. They cite the familiar figure of the Nazi concentration camp commander playing Mozart on the piano next door to the gas chambers to illustrate the limits of civilisation to act as a shield against barbarity.

The traditionalist's reply is that to expect EU functionaries armed with shibboleths of political correctness to tame malice and savagery impervious to Mozart and Mother Teresa is unrealistic. The destructive xenophobia of Hungary's far right is more reliably contained by the country's best traditions of national and Christian virtues. "It is good that you have come to us", Orbán said to the delegates, "because we need everyone's help and cooperation to successfully act against the spread of hate."

Don't hold your breath, Prime Minister. For "progressive" circles, helping centre-right governments is not on the agenda. Tainting centre-right governments with the brush of far-right ideas is much more the ticket. Is this because "progressive" circles, even Jewish ones, are like the Bourbon kings and can neither forget history nor learn from it — or are they just too traumatised to open their eyes? It would probably make no difference if they did open them. As Scruton puts it in his essay *The Need for Nations*: "The present Hungarian government, by making issues of national identity and national sentiment fundamental to its platform, has excited a strong and censorious response from the European Union, regardless of any other grounds for such disapproval."

Exactly, but how do you reassure those who remember history too well? How do you explain to people who fear ultranationalists for good reason that a moderate nationalist is not their problem but may be their solution? How do you tell a cat that burnt itself on the hot stove (that's Mark Twain's question) that it's okay to jump on a cold stove?

You can't. Some cats are smart and figure it out when Fido chases them. The ones that don't become a dog's breakfast.

THE VIEW FROM A SMALLER STATE

Péter Ákos Bod

It is not easy to take issue with Roger Scruton's analysis: his arguments on the need of nations are supported by his vast knowledge of history, ideas, politics and ethics, and by his impressive experience gained in various parts of our world, including pre- and post-transition East Central Europe. His intellectual arsenal would intimidate anyone wanting to question what he has to say about this complex subject. Yet, it is easy to take a very different position from his, for his short analysis brilliantly exposes the inherent contradictions of the modern world, the conflicting arguments of great thinkers of late, and the uncertainties surrounding the concepts of Europe, state and nation.

It is not easy to find fault with his essay which renders a powerful critique of the recent cult of multiculturalism and of the mainstream unilinear concept of progress. In this part of the world, one cannot but agree with him on the significance of national sentiments as a force legitimising the state, and a source of energy to do great things in historic times. Yet, it is easy to find counterarguments concerning the assumed constructive role of national sentiments in this very part of the world where nation building exercises have sometimes degenerated into suppression or forced assimilation of ethnic minorities, and these sentiments have frequently been played against other values.

It is not easy at all to question his thesis on the importance of the nation state, particularly in our part of the world where regaining state sovereignty has been the ultimate national goal of generations – along with an equally strong desire to get readmission to the "European family". In smaller states, this desire has been underpinned by a rational calculation of risks posed by powerful unfriendly nations and empires in the neighbourhood. It is however easy to take issue with the author who gets emotional about European integration and resorts to an un-British overstatement claiming that "In the current debt crisis the European elite – composed largely of the governing circles in France and Germany – has assumed the right to depose the elected governments of Greece and Italy, and to impose their own henchmen, chosen from the ranks of obedient apparatchiks".

The above-mentioned governments that have recently resigned amidst financial, moral and political crises are far from convincing arguments for unlimited national sovereignty; Berlusconi is a case in point, now struggling more with law and order institutions of his country than with the "European elite". But that is not the main issue. Where I find myself dissenting from Roger Scruton's argument is the nature of the link between European integration and national sovereignty of smaller states.

Before revisiting the issue of sovereignty, let us reflect on the viability of small states. As context, it is worth having a look at the map of Europe in 1900 – this is how I generally start my course on regime change and post-transition challenges. Even without actually looking at a history map, you will remember from your school years that pre-war Europe consisted of a few entities only: Great Britain; France, another colonial global player; Spain and Portugal as colonial powers already long in decline; the German Reich, stretching from Alsace to Konigsberg, what later became known as Kaliningrad; the Austro-Hungarian Monarchy; the Ottoman empire; Tsarist Russia, Italy, and some smaller entities on the periphery. This was the map in existence when my grandfather was born. On this map, you could not find *Poland* or *Ireland* or what we now call the *Baltic* republics. There existed the Nordic kingdoms and some dependent smaller southern states such as Romania, Serbia and Bulgaria, the latter with shaky finances and uncertain borders.

In that era, the monetary regime of Europe was straightforward: a dozen sovereigns with few currencies, most being on the gold standard. The small number of sizable European empires plus the kingdoms of Northern and Southern Europe all had their distinct legal systems, railway networks, and later national airlines. The European economies functioned well with a limited set of distinct technical standards and measurement systems, and a handful of official languages. In the age of industrial capitalism, *country size mattered*: under the production and technological conditions of the era, it was hard for smaller entities to be independent *and* advanced at the same time – *Switzerland* was a glaring exception. This era may be called the *age of nationalism*; but this is also the *age of mass production* with its "economies of scale". The viability of any entity with less than a dozen million of subjects was highly uncertain.

A hundred years later, in the year 2000, if you start reading the map of Europe west to east, it still looks pretty much the same, with some minor modifications of national borders, except for the emergence of independent Ireland. But look at Central and Eastern Europe! You will see a *new geography*: a series of new countries with new borders. The second map strikes you with a stark difference in respect of the *number of the sovereigns in Europe*: what was once only a province is now a sovereign republic. Ours is, in reality, the age of the nations!

But will small states remain viable in economic terms? Does it make economic sense to try to establish a sovereign state with only a couple of million subjects? The same issue is relevant on a European level: can a continent consisting of so many minor entities manage to stay competitive in face of lower cost challengers and high-tech competitors?

Imagine the absence of any form of European integration: all states, new and old, would have the right to their own currencies, health and industry standards, legal procedures and tax regulations. National parliaments could determine national voltage and rail gauge of their own. This vision – shared probably by a tenth of Europe's citizenry – would, if put into reality, lead to absurd consequences.

A look at the map of contemporary Europe, thus, makes most of us understand the objective necessity for sweeping harmonisation of rules, institutes and norms if new (and also older) member states desire to prosper. Small size of a national economy necessitates cross border trade of goods and services. Let us take *Estonia* as a case: its economy is smaller in terms of value generated than the economy of Lübeck, a German city; it would be absurd for the 1.3 million Estonians to attempt anything close to self-reliance. Economic and financial openness is a must for all new member states, even if having national borders and other requisites of national sovereignty is dear to the citizens and the elites of these states.

The new EU member states depend intensively on capital inflows. It must be so if they aspire to catch up with more advanced neighbours. And they all do aspire, very much. Market driven flows are sensitive to country risks as well as currency risks. That raises the obvious European issue of having national currencies. Does it make sense for every smallish state to print its own currency – what an American economist called "funny money"? A variety of national currencies would obviously lead to excessively high transaction costs in Europe; the existence of numerous monetary regimes increases uncertainties in financial matters. Conclusion: for economic prosperity, some sort of currency agreements – or a common currency – has to be created. I had once my signature as central bank governor on the Hungarian bank notes – which gives you a very special feeling when you pay in cash; so you can trust that I like Hungarian forint. Still my conviction is that we would have been better off with the euro. Now we are stuck with HUF and exchange rate volatility and external exposure to faceless markets.

The euro is admittedly a disputed issue. In the Europe of the pre-war era, the gold standard provided an adequate platform for free trade and smooth flow of capital; in today's Europe, which is made up of small to medium sized nations, international monetary and trade arrangements are more important than ever. You are right to object to the excesses of supranationality of the European integration process –

but let us also admit: the very existence of a number of European sovereign states is in no small measure due to Europe-wide harmonisation in legal, technological, institutional, financial and political matters.

So far I have touched upon money matters but one could equally take the issue of culture and language: small, and not that small, nations find some protection in the European project against the negative externalities emanating from what became known as globalisation. Think of the prospect of national film industries without legal and financial support of the EU, or the use of smaller languages. Mind you, all nations on the European continent can be regarded small in certain respects.

To cut my counterarguments short: *sovereignty* and *interdependence* are not mutually exclusive concepts. *Nation state* and limited sovereignty (*member state*) sound contradicting concepts but in real life you can sustain a workable *modus vivendi*. Being a *patriot* and being a *European* is also a duality that is not easy – but not impossible – to live with. Ask politicians on the periphery, and some will noisily complain in public, but talk to business people, artists, pensioners and students – and you will get mixed signals from the public. The young look at things differently: even football club loyalty, once a local and/or national issue, has been transformed into something new, as can be seen by the transnational fan bases of Barcelona, Milan, MU or Bayern. Polls indicate that this duality is less of a problem in good times and more when life is harder – and at present, we are experiencing rough times, mostly for economic and financial reasons.

The eurozone is certainly having deep problems – less the euro which is a remarkable noninflationary currency. You have read obituaries of the euro in British and American papers but the report of its death has been greatly exaggerated. Some of the eurozone's problems are caused by inner regulatory mistakes, others are due to serious mismanagement in some member states. National elites tend to blame "Brussels" for rules that governments of member states have set unitis viribus – and some countries have failed to keep. But that is politicking. Deeper down there are trends that create and recreate modalities to resolve the perennial contradiction between local and universal, national and European. Muddling through, yes – this is the best the continent seems to offer as crisis strategy. But it is still better than getting stuck in oriental mud.

THE NEED FOR SATISFIED
NATIONAL MINORITIES

Géza Jeszenszky

It is both a revelation and a delight to read such an unorthodox essay as Roger Scruton's "The Need for Nations". The author is absolutely right to point out that "nation states [...] alone inspire the obedience of the European people, and without them there is no way that the machinery of the Union can act. [...] National loyalty marginalises loyalties of family, tribe and faith, and places before the citizen's eyes, as the focus of his patriotic feeling, not a person or a group but a country. This country is defined by a territory, and by the history, culture and law that have made that territory *ours*. It is the emergence of territory from behind religion, tribe and dynasty that characterises the nationalist art and literature of the 19th century..." The uncommon view that the European Union cannot supplant national loyalties by a supranational "European" loyalty is fully supported by the recent financial crisis and its aftermath.

The national idea ("nationalism") became the dominant ideology of the 19th century, and in the 20th it led to the break-up of the multinational Russian, Ottoman and Habsburg Empires. But the new countries emerging out of the ruins of the Empires were a far cry from being genuine nation states. The ethnic mixture of Central and South-Eastern Europe precluded the drawing of ethnic borders.[1] Strategic and economic considerations awarding some and punishing other nations loaded almost all the new states with millions of unhappy and hostile national minorities. Those minorities made up almost a third of the population of the territory between the Germans and the Russians. Hitler and Stalin managed to reduce their proportion considerably by murder and mass expulsions (called transfers) to about 10 per cent of the overall population. Then in the 1990s the artificial Yugoslav, Soviet and Czechoslovak federations broke up – the first amid a horrible war, the two others surprisingly peacefully. But even that did not lead to more homogeneous states, commanding the loyalty and dedication of all the citizens. On the contrary, in the Balkans and in the post-Soviet space millions of new national minorities were created. 25 million Russians found themselves outside the borders of the Russian Federation (which continued to include millions of non-Russians), while hundreds of thousands of Albanians, Serbs, Croats and Romanians are minorities in the successor states of Yugoslavia. The new political map did not ease the situation (and mistreatment) of 2.5 million Hungarians cut off from their native land by the 1920 "Bad Treaty That Won't Go Away" (the title of an essay by the renowned concert pianist Bálint Vázsonyi), neither that of the Poles in Lithuania and Belarus. German, Lithuanian, Slovak, Bulgarian, Greek, Turkish and other national minorities add to the complexity of the issue. (Some of the minorities passed from one citizenship to another several times in one lifetime.)

Here I do not want to raise the infinite problems presented by the "new", predominantly non-European minorities who have inundated Western Europe in the last fifty years. My concern is the equally serious issue of the autochthonous "historical" or "national" minorities in the formerly communist-dominated countries, in the new members of the European Union. The media and the political leaders pay very little attention to their disadvantageous position, to the denial of the modest rights internal and international legislation provides them, and to the many tensions and conflicts resulting from the intolerance of the majority national group. It is high time to realise that in most multiethnic countries, and in Central and Eastern Europe particularly, ethnicity, religion and language are the source of primary loyalty, and they are the basis of the nations. The fashionable western ideal, an integrated multiethnic society where the majority national group does not aim at undermining the position and reducing the size of the national minorities, has no appeal here, at least not to the majority national group. In the eastern half of Europe the State has traditionally not been neutral in matters concerning language and culture, it rather served as a tool for the harassment of the national minorities, in the futile hope that the ethnically heterogeneous population can be "homogenised", assimilated, and thus the nominal nation states can become real nation states. These countries are not melting pots; the present national minorities emerged not by people crossing borders but by borders crossing people. Attempts to turn this region into a melting pot can transform it into a powder keg, as older and most recent history amply testifies.

This situation is not confined to Europe, in fact most of the states of Asia and Africa are also multinational, and the serious mistreatment and oppression of the various ethnic and religious minorities is all too common. But States which try to build a centralising system are experiencing an upsurge of separatist movements. Nigeria, Congo and Sri Lanka are only some of the most obvious examples. In Afghanistan, "nation building" is hardly possible, because there is no such thing as an Afghan nation, there are only Pashtun, Uzbek, Tajik, Hazara etc. tribal territories (usually overlapping), with co-nationals living in the neighbouring states. On the other hand India, South Africa, Kenya, even Pakistan are more promising cases, mainly on account of the fact that those states recognise the separate identities of the various regions, historical provinces and national groups. Which direction Myanmar (Burma) will take is still uncertain. But it can be safely stated that *one of the key problems facing the world is finding a way for the harmonious coexistence and collaboration of the many national/ethnic/religious groups living together in one state.* As a most important Resolution of the Council of Europe states, "Most of the present conflicts can often be traced to the dichotomy between the principle of the indivisibility of states and the principle of identity, and are rooted in tensions between states and minority groups which demand the right to preserve their identities."[2] It is a sad symptom of present-day Europe that no action was taken in connection with that Resolution; it has remained a dead letter. I hope to show in a forthcoming essay that the lot of millions of national minorities in Central and Eastern Europe is unacceptable and continues to threaten the stability of Europe. (The European Stability Pact of 1995 was well meant but it had no effect whatsoever.)

Despite the present relatively low prestige of the European Union it is the most important achievement of the second half of the 20th century. It should be improved, not discarded. It speaks so much about values, why is it dumb on the rights of the national minorities? It has many thousand pages of rules and regulations, but there is not even talk about expanding them towards minority rights. The EU is not dumb on Roma rights, that is fine, but ending discrimination and intolerance towards the national minorities is far easier than lifting millions of Roma from poverty and ignorance. If the EU politely passes the issue to the OSCE or the Council of Europe then we face the familiar problem of lack of means for enforcing the existing – admittedly rather mild – conventions and recommendations.

European integration, the spirit of tolerance and the adoption of binding conventions promised a solution, or at least a serious alleviation to the problem of the national minorities. Reconciliation between old adversaries, the gradual "spiritualisation" of international borders in Europe, the free movement of people in addition to capital and goods became a reality in the Common Market. It was a perspective that inspired many who lived on the wrong side of the Iron Curtain.

After the collapse of communism the EU and NATO had great influence over all the countries that aspired for membership in those organisations. That influence could have been used to induce governments to guarantee the rights and interests of the national minorities through decentralisation or "devolution". European integration was envisaged to go hand-in-hand with regionalism. But apparently a Hungarian region in Romania and in Slovakia is still anathema for the majority people.

One thing is certain I am afraid. The issue of the national and ethnic minorities is a time bomb which threatens to explode. A preventive solution must be found, combining national legislation and enlightened practice with international action like the codification of rights, monitoring their observance and a mechanism of enforcement. Minorities need guarantees for a decent life and a future. Individual minority rights are not enough. It is often argued that there is no such thing as collective rights or group rights for minorities. Although both the UN (in Article 27 in the International Covenant on Civil and Political Rights) and the Council of Europe (most explicitly in the 1993 Recommendation 1201 of its Parliamentary Assembly) speaks of rights that could be exercised "in community with others in their group" and states that local self-government is desirable, most European countries do not endorse the idea. But no one denies that xenophobia and racial discrimination exist. Those prejudices are seldom directed at an individual but rather at people as the member(s) of a particular ethnic or religious group or community. If the denial of rights takes place on a collective basis, then positive legal guarantees should be also available for a whole community.

The future EU should indeed be built on nations and on states with satisfied national minorities.

---

[1] Two contemporary experts' testimony: "the various nationalities of Central Europe are so interlocked, and their racial frontiers are so unsuitable as the frontiers of really independent sovereign states..." Memorandum by L.S. Amery, "The Austro-Hungarian Problem", 20 October 1918. Public Record Office (London), Foreign Office, 371/3136/17223; "The Commission is forced to the conclusion that the frontiers proposed are unsatisfactory as the international boundaries of sovereign states. It has been found impossible to discover such lines, which would be at the same time just and practical." Charles Seymour, "Epitome of Reports on Just and Practical Boundaries Within Austria-Hungary for Czecho-Slovaks, Jugo-Slavs, Rumanians, Poles, Ruthenians, Magyars", undated [around the end of 1918], National Archives (Washington), RG 256. Inquiry Doc. 514.

[2] Resolution 1334 (2003). Positive experiences of autonomous regions as a source of inspiration for conflict resolution in Europe.
http://assembly.coe.int/Main.asp?link=/Documents/AdoptedText/ta03/ERES1334.htm

REGIME CHANGE IN HUNGARY, 1990–1994: THE ECONOMIC POLICIES OF THE ANTALL GOVERNMENT

Ottó Hieronymi

REGIME CHANGE: THE NATURE OF THE CHALLENGE AND THE RECORD OF THE ANTALL GOVERNMENT

The collapse of the communist regime was one of the most important positive developments of the twentieth century, a century full of crises and tragedies. For Hungary, as for other communist countries including the Soviet Union, this represented a great opportunity as well as a serious challenge.

The challenge can be summed up in simple terms: how to build a stable democracy and a prosperous market economy on the ruins left by an oppressive, inefficient and corrupt political and economic system. This challenge was amplified by the legitimate desire of the populations of the former communist countries to catch up as rapidly as possible with the prosperity of the countries of the free Western world – a world that they were finally able to join.

József Antall, the first freely elected Prime Minister of Hungary, was fully aware of this opportunity and of the challenge that it represented. He was aware of the unique historic responsibility of his office and of his government. This sense of responsibility was one of the hallmarks of his statesmanship – a statesmanship recognised by all the leaders of the established democracies who came to know him. It was also the sense of responsibility that he wanted to leave as his legacy, after his untimely death, to his successors and fellow politicians, and to the Hungarian people.

More than two decades after the collapse of the communist system the experience of the economic policies of the Antall government is of more than historical interest. This experience is relevant for the debates about the current economic situation in Hungary and about the policies adopted by earlier post-Antall governments. The lessons from the Hungarian experience of the early 1990s are relevant also in a broader context as political leaders and experts in Europe and in the rest of OECD area are seeking a way out of a profound fiscal, monetary and economic crisis.

Much has been written about Antall and the "Antall years", perhaps not enough by those who had been close to him and who were familiar not only with the quality of his political thought but also with his unique ability to steer Hungary through the exciting but difficult years of the "regime change".

There is no doubt that the policies of the Antall government were far from perfect. The "trial and error" approach, the struggle of the governments of the rich and "established" democracies to overcome the consequences of the financial crisis, and the repeated errors of commission and omission of the leaders of the Western market economies are proof enough that economic policy and economic reform are not easy tasks even under normal circumstances – i.e. when no change of system or "regime change" is involved.

Yet the main conclusions are positive. They can be summed up in three points.

In the first place, with the passing of time, the objectives and policies in the economic area of the Antall government look better and better each year in the light of the record of the various post-Antall governments and the current situation of the Hungarian economy.

The second point is that, contrary to a widely held misconception that the Prime Minister was not interested in economics, Antall was very much aware of the importance of economic policy. The thrust of the government's policies reflected his values and convictions and analyses, shared by key members of his government and by his close advisers. He had a clear sense of objectives and priorities, and he was the leader and initiator also in this field. While many brandished different views at the time, the Antall government had a consistent and balanced concept and approach both in the short-term crisis management of the economy that had been left on the brink of bankruptcy by the preceding regime, and with respect to long-term reconstruction and the development of the market economy. This basic concept and approach continued to inform the legislative program and the policies of the government throughout its four-year term.

Finally, some initiatives by Prime Minister Antall and by his government, even if they did not succeed because of the lack of domestic or external support, went without question in the right direction. Over the years it has become increasingly clear that the break with this balanced concept and approach, by the successive Socialist–Liberal coalitions, has created more serious problems for the Hungarian economy than the policies pursued during the initial four years of "regime change" between 1990 and 1994. This became especially evident in the wake of the outbreak in 2008 of the worldwide financial crisis.

Three examples are discussed in the rest of this article to support and to illustrate the above conclusions: (1) the economic and social model ("the social market economy"), (2) the issue of the external debt, (3) the strategy of bank privatisation.

Other major relevant topics, such as the role of the Working Group on Economic Strategy (GAM), the overall record of privatisation and the assessment of the "economic and social legacy of 40 years of the communist system", a project that was undertaken on the personal initiative of Prime Minister Antall in 1993 and was completed only after his death, will be discussed in a later article.

THE "ECONOMIC AND SOCIETAL MODEL": THE GOAL OF THE "SOCIAL MARKET ECONOMY"

The model chosen by the Hungarian Democratic Forum and its leader József Antall for the transformation of the socialist economy into a modern market economy was that of the "social market economy".

The choice of this model was easy to understand. The "social market economy" had been by far the most successful model of reconstruction and economic transformation after the Second World War. It combined growth and stability, social progress and competition and efficiency. Nevertheless, Hungary turned out to be the only former communist country (in addition obviously to the German Democratic Republic) that attempted to adopt "the social market economy" as the model for its future economic and social order.

There was little understanding for this choice among "international experts" – not only in the US or Britain, but even in continental Europe. In the international organisations that claimed economic policy expertise, there was neither knowledge of, nor interest for what the "social market economy" was about. These included the IMF, the IBRD, the UNCTAD, the OECD and the European Commission. This was also true for the European Bank for Reconstruction and Development that was created specifically to help the "transition" of former communist countries towards a "European-type" market economy. Strangely enough, even the German Minister of Finance, Theo Waigel, argued that the social market economy was not an "export model".

Yet today there is a broad consensus throughout Europe, inside and outside Germany, that the current deep crisis could have been avoided if the principles of the social market economy had been followed more systematically by the members of the European Union.

Neither economists nor policy makers seem to have noticed or they have forgotten that the German model is already enshrined in the basic objectives of the EU. According to Article 3 of the Lisbon Treaty: "The Union shall establish an internal market. It shall work for the sustainable development of Europe based on balanced economic growth and price stability, a highly competitive *social market economy,* aiming at full employment and social progress, and a high level of protection and improvement of the quality of the environment." (Emphasis added.)

THE EXTERNAL DEBT PROBLEM

Among the former communist countries in Eastern Europe, Hungary had the highest per capita external debt and the highest annual debt service. The heavy external debt burden represented one of the principal constraints on the new government's policy options. It was rightly seen as a brake on both investments and on private consumption. It was also one of the sources of the macro-economic imbalances in the Hungarian economy and of the recurring refrain: we not only need conservative fiscal and monetary policies, but we also have "to love austerity" in order to avoid provoking nervous reactions by creditors, which increase the financing costs and the debt burden.

The large external debt that Hungary had accumulated by the end of the 1980s (a number that was a state secret – and the Western governments, international organisations and banks obliged the Hungarian communist government by keeping the information secret) reflected the mismanagement of the Hungarian economy and had a snowballing effect since during the 1980s a significant part of the debt service was turned into principal.

The super-salesman of Hungary's creditworthiness was János Fekete, the long-serving Vice-President of the Hungarian National Bank under the Kádár regime, who was *ad personam* a member (the only one from the communist world) of the Group of Thirty, a select group of international monetary and financial leaders. Fekete could speak as fluently and convincingly the jargon of the Wall Street international bankers and reassure the markets about Hungary's commitment to market reform, as he could speak the language of the senior communist apparatchik (that he was) to reassure not only the Head of the Hungarian Communist Party, János Kádár, but also the leaders in the Kremlin about the solid future of communism in Hungary.

Indirectly, the size of the Hungarian debt was also the result of the so-called "Volcker shock" which reversed the American inflation and the downward slide of the US dollar of the 1970s. This was compounded by the way "the international community" decided, following the Mexican crisis of 1982, to shift most of the burden of dealing with the "international debt crisis" on the shoulders of the borrowers instead of effectively sharing it with the equally responsible lenders (the international banks) and their home governments (and the international organisations, like the IMF, which had been applauding during the 1970s the "successful recycling of the petrodollars").

The recipe was a combination of rescheduling of official or officially guaranteed debt and putting pressure on the debtor countries to adopt austerity policies and to carry out "structural adjustment programme". In many respects these were overdue, but the idea that the debtor countries should bear alone the consequences of the irresponsible "recycling of the petrodollars" was short-sighted both from an economic and political point of view. There was no trace of an effective burden-sharing in the programmes that carried the name of two Republican Secretaries of the Treasury: the Baker Plan and the Brady Plan.

For the Antall government the external debt was one of the most visible but also one of the heaviest parts of the legacy of 40 years of communism. Should the debt inherited from the Kádár regime be repudiated? Should the government ask for a moratorium, for a debt reduction or should it even declare an outright bankruptcy? What were the costs and consequences of such a measure? What were the possible alternatives?

Prime Minister Antall and his team were convinced of the need to try to obtain a reduction of the debt burden, both in the servicing of the debt and in the principal. They were, however, also aware of the risks, for both the international position of Hungary and the domestic situation, in the case of a unilateral move on the debt issue.

Clearly the risks were judged to be higher than the benefits that could be expected even under a "best case scenario". This conclusion was correct not only in the light of the record of the "international debt crisis" of the 1980s and of the outcome of the Baker and Brady Plans. It has also been proven correct by events posterior to 1990: the outcome of the Polish and the Yugoslav financial and monetary crises and collapse, as well as the international financial crises of the last 20 years, including the latest ones, Greece and Cyprus.

There was a consensus within the Antall government that if a financial collapse was to be avoided, Western governments ought to share the responsibility for a move on the debt issue, and this should be backed up by a clear commitment to assume the burden of debt reduction. Without such a guarantee Hungary would have been facing its creditors without the least hope for a rapid negotiated settlement. Yet, the negotiation of such a settlement would have had to be rapid and conclusive in order to avoid a financial panic. This would have affected not only the domestic and external value of the forint but also severely constrained the financing of imports and the very functioning of an already fragile economy.

However, when US Treasury officials of the (first) Bush administration were asked whether a different approach from that of the 1980s could be adopted for the former communist economies (in the light of the major contributions of some of these countries to the collapse of the communist system), the reactions ranged from suggestions that the best solution was a unilateral suspension of payments (which would lead to a temporary reduction of Hungary's debt service but not of the principal), or as was the case with Secretary Brady, a simple refusal to hear the question and to discuss the issue.

The reluctance of the Antall government to adopt a unilateral debt strategy was also reinforced by the lack of support that such a strategy would have received from the bureaucracy of the Ministry of Finance and of the National Bank of Hungary or from the bureaucracy of the IMF or the World Bank.

In the light of the poor performance of the international financial institutions during the 1970s (recycling of the petrodollars) and the subsequent debt crisis of the 1980s, little economic understanding and political sympathy could be expected from the IMF or from the World Bank – two organisations that claimed leading roles in guiding the "transition process" in Eastern Europe.

In countless discussions at the level of the "working staff" and of the members of the governing bodies of these two institutions there was a systematic refusal to discuss the "resource shortage" in the former communist countries and how this resource shortage was being aggravated by the international banking and financial system. International bureaucrats systematically argued that "private capital could do the job". They showed no knowledge or acknowledgement of the historical precedents of the successful reconstruction experience in Western Europe and in Japan after the Second World War, nor a willingness to discuss the one exception in the wake of the collapse of the communist system, i.e. the burden-sharing involved in the process of German reunification – not only between the "old" and the "new" *Länder* of the Federal Republic, but also between the EC/EU and Germany.

The direct and indirect aid from the EC/EU granted to the 17 million citizens of the former German Democratic Republic was more than the total direct aid to all the other former members of the COMECON. The short-sightedness and the cynicism of some of the international civil servants can be illustrated by the comment of one of them on this discrepancy: "*Sonderfall Deutschland*" – "Germany is a special case". To this arrogant statement this official (who happened to be German) added "At any rate, a country like Hungary could not absorb any significant official resource transfers to help build the market economy" (!).

BILATERAL ATTEMPTS

The question "could Hungary hope to receive a non-debt-creating transfer of resources (other than through privatisation)", as finally and belatedly occurred once it became a member of the EU, was never off the agenda of József Antall and of his close staff and advisers. This was not only an economic and financial issue but also a political and moral one. The Prime Minister felt that he and his government owed it to the Hungarian people not to give up trying.

With bankruptcy discarded because of its direct and indirect consequences and the multilateral road blocked by both "conventional wisdom" and the international bureaucracy, the one remaining option to be explored was the bilateral one.

The first attempt took place in the immediate aftermath of the "taxi blockade". The paralysis of virtually all traffic and as a result of the entire economy by a coordinated blockade by taxi drivers following an adjustment of the price of gasoline created considerable concern in Western and in particular European capitals.

In Bonn Chancellor Kohl feared that this extremely-well coordinated anti-government action would destabilise the Hungarian government and the new democracy, especially at a time when the Prime Minister was hospitalised, undergoing major surgery and post-surgery treatment. The threat of a government crisis was also increased by a speech and by the behind the scenes agitation of President Göncz. The President made the government's task more difficult by taking the side of the organisers of the blockade, urging the authorities to cancel the increase in fuel prices and suggesting the creation of a "grand coalition".

Chancellor Kohl decided to send to Budapest a large delegation of German officials to offer political, psychological and material help to the "beleaguered" Hungarian government, and also to take the pulse of the political actors. The German delegation was led by Otto Schlecht, State Secretary in the Ministry of Economics, who had been for many years a close collaborator of the late Ludwig Erhard, the "father of the German economic miracle".

At the plenary meeting of the two delegations made up of Hungarian and German officials, the head of the Hungarian delegation went straight to the point: if the

European countries wanted to strengthen the political support of the market economy, among the Hungarian population, they would have to make a concrete gesture to ease the costs of transition from communism to the market economy. A realistic number would be $3 billion over a period of three years (one billion per year, beginning in 1991). This transfer would be used under the supervision of the donor countries for modernising infrastructure, social investments, loan consolidation, etc.

Over dinner, this proposal was discussed with Schlecht, who was probably the Western high official who knew most intimately from both the 1948–52 period and from the generous transfers into East Germany, how much such a gesture would have given a boost to democracy and to the market economy, and how much it would have been compatible with the tradition and the spirit of the social market economy. Schlecht listened politely. Early next morning the German delegation left for Bonn and there was no response to this Hungarian proposal, except for relatively modest credits to finance the shipment of brown coal from East Germany that could no longer be used in Germany because of the more stringent environmental controls in the Federal Republic. For Hungary it was deemed to be good enough.

The second major attempt at "bilateral persuasion" was prepared from early 1991 onwards (with the full approval of the "Economic Cabinet"). A detailed note was prepared to illustrate the "resource shortage" in Hungary and how a transfer of $3 billion could facilitate the success of the Hungarian transformation. This was important because there was a tendency to underestimate the costs of transition and the difficult conditions in which Hungary was left after the collapse of the communist regime.

Prime Minister Antall accepted to take this message to Chancellor Kohl with the request that he submit it to the members of the G7 prior to their London summit. After the Antall–Kohl meeting there was no more news about this request than there had been about the previous one.

Beside praise for the IMF and for the World Bank and congratulations for the creation of the EBRD, the economic problems of the new democracies received scant attention at the 1991 summit meeting of the G7. The final communiqué had this to say:

"We salute the courage and determination of the countries of Central and Eastern Europe in building democracy and moving to market economies, despite formidable obstacles. We welcome the spread of political and economic reform throughout the region. These changes are of great historical importance. Bulgaria and Romania are now following the pioneering advances of Poland, Hungary and Czechoslovakia. Albania is emerging from its long isolation. (We recognise) that successful reform depends principally on the continuing efforts of the countries concerned..."

For the record it should be mentioned that the Clinton administration was no more perceptive about the economic situation and problems in Eastern Europe than its predecessor, the Bush administration. Thus, for example Larry Summers, at the time number two in the US Treasury (later to be promoted to the position of Secretary of the Treasury) declared at the 1994 Annual Meeting of the EBRD that all the former communist countries ought to take Albania as their model for its allegedly deep commitment to the principles of the modern market economy. (This exhortation was made not long before the virtual collapse of the Albanian economy as a result of a Ponzi scheme.)

The conclusion that the Fall 1990 initiative and the Memorandum for the G7 governments were not naïve "fishing expeditions" can be supported by at least four strong arguments: (1) the record of the 1948–1952 American aid programme to help reconstruction ("Marshall Plan"), (2) the size of the direct aid transferred from the "old" to the "new" *Bundesländer*, (3) the enormous costs of the failure of "regime change" in former Yugoslavia and parts of the former Soviet Union not only for the population of the countries but also for Europe and the Western World as a whole, and finally (4) what should have been the realisation of how much was at stake in the success or failure of the regime change. Even before having lived through the Yugoslav nightmare, it should have been clear to European (and also American) leaders, both from logic and from historical experience, that prevention of failure is less onerous and more rewarding than trying to deal with the aftermath of economic and financial collapse.

German statistics (just like EU or American statistics) are not very transparent when it comes to foreign aid and even for transfer payments within the same country. It is always politically safer to provide lower figures and to hide some transactions under headings that are relatively difficult to interpret. This is also clearly the case with West Germany's (and of the other EU members') direct or indirect payments for the reconstruction of East Germany. Still, the total amount over a 15 year period is reliably estimated to have exceeded DM1500 billion (or roughly the equivalent today of $1.5 trillion). The net debt accumulated by the German privatisation agency alone amounted to more than DM200 billion after four years of activity.

The Antall government's debt strategy also had some positive aspects and consequences. First and foremost it helped avoid an international and domestic financial crisis. The economic and social consequences of such breakdowns were illustrated by the case of the Yugoslav economy – prior to the country's break-up –, Poland as well as the Russian Federation. Also, this policy contributed to encouraging private direct investments and the modernisation of Hungarian industry and service sectors. Lastly, Hungary was in principle better equipped to deal on a more equal basis with the experts and the high officials of the IMF and the World Bank and the newly created EBRD (which suffered from the same myopia as the two principal Bretton Woods institutions). That the Hungarian governments that followed the Antall government were not always very skilful in using and preserving this moral and monetary capital was their fault and not the fault of Prime Minister Antall and his government.

THE STRATEGY OF BANK PRIVATISATION

The last issue to be mentioned briefly in this article is the Antall government's strategy of bank privatisation.

It should be mentioned here that among the former communist countries Hungary under the Antall government adhered most closely to the principle of market privatisation. For Prime Minister Antall it was important, for economic, political and ethical reasons to avoid the "mirror image" of what happened during the nationalisations in the 1940s, i.e. the wasteful expropriation of private assets. This time it would have been the wasteful distribution of public assets without payments. Market-driven privatisation meant selling to both Hungarian and foreign investors. The two principal criteria were (1) the price that could be obtained and (2) the outlook for modernising the privatised companies and improving their competitive position on the domestic and international markets.

The government retained the right to define special conditions and strategies for the privatisation of key sectors of the national economy. One of the principal examples in this category was the strategy of bank privatisation.

The detailed bank privatisation strategy was adopted in the spring of 1992. Two key points from this strategy were:

> the requirement that the balance sheets of the banks had to be cleaned up before privatisation could start and that the cost of this cleaning up could not be charged to the banks' current and future clients;

> leading international banks were to be sought as strategic partners in the large Hungarian banks, but "at the same time it (was) important to avoid that the Hungarian banking system should come under foreign control".

The timing of the strategy would have allowed that at least one or two, or even three of the large Hungarian banks could have concluded a strategic partnership with major international banks well before the end of the mandate of the government. Yet this strategy suffered serious delays for a number of domestic and international reasons virtually from the start.

A first factor was the systematic opposition by the Ministry of Finance (and by some of the Hungarian bankers, most prominent among whom was the head of the Budapest Bank, who later became Minister of Finance in the Horn government) and their delaying tactics to the creation of a loan consolidation fund, which was necessary to clean up the banks' balance sheets. Since there was no hope for official external financing, the projected fiscal impact of this policy was a useful pretext for those who rejected the strategy from the start, essentially because it was coming from the Antall government.

The second major problem was the desire or even the explicit insistence of foreign governments (in particular of the US and the UK) and of the EU Commission and the World Bank that they should have a direct involvement in and virtual control of the Hungarian bank privatisation process. When it was made clear to them that the bank privatisation process was the exclusive responsibility of the Hungarian government, the EU Commission, the US AID and the British government immediately went back on their earlier commitments to help finance the costly process of bank privatisation (it was understood that this would have paid the bills of the Western investment banks who would advise the Hungarian government). There were few more blatant examples of interference with the sovereignty of the Hungarian government by Western countries and organisations during the years of the Antall government.

As a result, no major banks were privatised during the term in office of the Antall government. Thus, the second requirement of the strategy mentioned above, i.e. the "finding of major strategic partners for the large Hungarian banks without allowing the Hungarian banking system to come under foreign control" was never put to a true feasibility test. Of course, if this strategy (international opening but no foreign domination of the banks) had been upheld by subsequent Hungarian governments, it might have run afoul of an ideological veto from Brussels, and, as the case of Italy shows it even could have led to criminal prosecution of the officials trying to implement this strategy.

Many people remember the case of the unfortunate Antonio Fazio, long-serving and highly respected Governor of the Italian central bank. (It should be noted that the officers of the *Banca d'Italia* were internationally known as being highly professional and the least corruptible in Italy.) In 2005 Fazio had to resign because of criminal charges (based on wiretaps), that he was using his position to prevent the takeover of an Italian bank by a foreign bank. In fact, it had long been suspected that Fazio was not sufficiently enthusiastic about the ideology and practice of the merger and take-over mania that prevailed in the banking sector in Europe and in the world at large, and that he was not happy with the prospect that this trend could lead to "foreign control of the Italian banking sector".

The foreign bank in the case that destroyed Mr Fazio's professional career and personal honour and reputation was the Dutch bank ABN Amro. According to Shakespeare "all is well that ends well": in 2006, under the governorship of Fazio's successor, Mario Draghi (who happens to be the current Head of the European Central Bank), ABN Amro obtained what it had sought vainly before the demise of Fazio. But unfortunately the story did not end at this point. This happened to be especially unfortunate not only for ABN Amro, but also for the Dutch, British and Belgian taxpayers and savers and for the entire European banking system. In fact, ABN Amro – the second largest Dutch bank – shortly after its Italian adventure became involved in a much bigger and much more complex M&A operation where it came under the ultimate control of the Royal Bank of Scotland.

And this was still not the end of the story. Virtually "before the ink was dry" on the signatures of the legal documents and well before the complex structure of the new European mega bank became fully operational and could deliver on the traditional optimistic promises of future gains of synergy, efficiency and profitability contained in the merger documents, the world was hit by the international financial crises.

As everyone knows by now, the case of "Royal Bank of Scotland & ABN Amro" became one of the prime examples and symbols for all that had been wrong with mega mergers among banks, with rootless banking giants and their contempt for ordinary commercial borrowers (and savers), and ultimately with their false sense of security that they are "too big to fail" and for the official policies that had encouraged and condoned these trends.

With all this hindsight and in the full knowledge of the consequences of the financial crisis and with widespread concern about what may still lie ahead, is it not fair to say that the prudence shown both in the bank privatisation strategy of the Antall government and in the preoccupations of Governor Fazio was to a large extent justified even if it went against the *Zeitgeist*, the spirit of the time?

COMRADE BARON

A Journey Through the Vanishing World of the Transylvanian Aristocracy
(Excerpt)

Jaap Scholten

Following the resounding success of the Dutch original, Jaap Scholten'n Comrade Baron *has been published in English, too. We are re-printing here a passage selected by the author from the new release by Corvina Press of Budapest. The archival photos are not taken from the Corvina edition.*

AFTER HIS DEATH, WAGONLOADS OF BOOKS KEPT ARRIVING

Marosvásárhely, March 2009

I step through a large door into the Teleki Téka[1]. Count Sámuel Teleki (1739–1822) founded this library and donated it to the town of Marosvásárhely. A white, U-shaped building, it has an arched gallery on the first floor reminiscent of a cloister. I climb a flight of stone steps and knock on a door. Beyond lies a long room with tables covered in papers and books. There are three women and one man. The man seems disturbed by my arrival. A young woman with black curly hair hurries towards me when I tell her I've come for the Teleki Téka. She has a giant key in her hand, as if for a medieval town gate. She's a specialist in medieval Transylvanian nobility.

In the 1950s several of Count Sámuel Teleki's direct descendants lived somewhere in this building. I suppose it ought to be seen as evidence of the charitableness of the communist system that they were permitted a bolt-hole. The space was so small that one of the Telekis slept on top of a cupboard.

I ask the woman whether she's heard of Gemma Teleki. Perhaps she knows where she lived? Certainly. She turns round and points to a side door, which opens onto a dark, dead-end corridor about five metres long and a metre and a half wide. It's the kind of space in which you would store cardboard boxes that might come in handy one day, empty bottles for the deposit, or a bicycle with a flat tyre. Here Gemma Teleki lived with two other Telekis. People who knew her well have told me that Gemma was an exceptional person, very intelligent, perhaps too intelligent for her own good.

My guide opens a tall door. After crossing a hallway we find ourselves in a large room. She turns on the lights. Since 1802, the year the library opened, nothing here has changed, except that there is electricity now. An inner sanctum. The windows have shutters. The bookcases are painted white and their doors have chicken wire instead of glass. The space is two storeys high; the upper-level walkway is lined with bookcases on all four walls. At the far end of the room hangs a large portrait of Sámuel Teleki as chancellor of Transylvania, an ermine robe over his shoulders and a sceptre in his hand. He is flanked by portraits of the two other noblemen who founded large libraries in Transylvania: Sámuel Brukenthal and Ignatius Batthyány.

On the wall is a map of Europe showing the twenty-five cities from which Teleki assembled his collection. They include Amsterdam, Leiden, Utrecht and Rotterdam, as well as Zurich, Padua, Rome, Leipzig, Ulm, Budapest and Pécs. He had contacts in all those cities, dealers and buyers searching on his behalf. Over his lifetime Teleki compiled a collection of 40,000 books. After his death in 1822, wagonloads of books kept arriving in Marosvásárhely.

Ninety-one-year-old Erzsébet T. has told me that many Transylvanian nobles attended universities in the Netherlands. One of her ancestors studied at Utrecht and some of his letters have survived. From Transylvania and Hungary they usually travelled by boat along the Polish and German rivers to the Baltic, and from there they walked to the Netherlands.

In the sixteenth and seventeenth centuries, around three thousand Transylvanians and Hungarians studied in the Netherlands, including 1,233 in Franeker, 740 in Utrecht and 655 in Leiden. Among them were sons of the powerful Transylvanian families. Erzsébet says that the son of an aristocrat was usually accompanied by two capable but penniless students from the village or surrounding district. The aristocrat's family would pay the two villagers' tuition fees and living expenses. In 1692 Mihály Bethlen went to Franeker, as did Pál Teleki in 1696.

Wolfgangus Bánffy (known in Hungary as Farkas Bánffy) arrived in Leiden in 1747 to study theology and Joseph Teleki followed in 1760. Until the late eighteenth century, Protestants were not allowed to attend universities in the Habsburg Empire. If they studied there nevertheless, they would not be awarded a degree.

A few years ago I gave a series of lectures at the Dutch faculty of the Eötvös Loránd University in Budapest. At the first lecture I asked my students why they had decided to study Dutch. One of them, who was from Transylvania, said she'd chosen the course because she'd inherited her Transylvanian grandfather's Dutch library.

The aristocracy was essential to the dissemination of culture in Transylvania, and indeed in Hungary, founding academies, opera houses, theatres, libraries, spas, museums and arboreta. Sámuel Teleki was the prototype of this kind of patron. He studied at Utrecht, Leiden, Basel and Paris, and for the rest of his life he was influenced by the ideas of the Enlightenment. He developed an overwhelming desire to found a large library in Transylvania. The collection is still almost entirely intact, with fifty-two incunabula as well as rare works that include prints by Rubens, Dürer, Cranach and Holbein, and tomes featuring signed engravings by Giovanni Battista and Francesco Piranesi. He attempted to build up a broad collection in which both the humanities – theology, philosophy, jurisprudence – and the natural sciences were represented. The works range across time from Aristotle to Rousseau, including books by Luther and Calvin (as with most of Transylvania's aristocrats, nine out of ten Telekis were Protestants), and by Thomasius, Kepler and Newton.

The aristocrats of Hungary and Transylvania were traditionally patrons to new poets and writers. In the seventeenth century the diaries and memoirs of the nobles themselves were the region's most important literary expression. They alone had the time and opportunity to read and write. Virtually everyone else worked on the land.

János Kemény (prince of Transylvania from 1660 to 1662) was seized by the Tartars and taken to the Crimea. During his imprisonment there he compiled the first memoir ever written in Hungarian, and in it he says a great deal about Transylvania. The tradition of writing memoirs continues to this day. Ilona's grandfather wrote an account of his life entitled *Hier bin ich geboren* (This is where I was born). The grandfather of one of the Transylvanians I spoke to had made three handwritten copies of his life story under communism, like a monk. He describes all the property confiscated from the family, with drawings of roads, railway lines, villages and family estates. Based on those drawings, his grandson was able to specify exactly which properties in Romania the state was legally bound to return to him.

For centuries foreign authors had a huge impact on Hungarian literature and philosophy, in part because Hungarian nobles living in exile produced so much literature, such as Ferenc Rákóczi II, whose autobiographical work was influenced by Fénelon and Rabelais. The aristocracy often took its lead from the French Enlightenment. Francophile Transylvanian Count László Haller translated Fénelon's *Télémaque* and Hungarian Count Fekete corresponded with Voltaire.

Interest in French Enlightenment thought was even greater in Transylvania, where for centuries there had been a bond with France as an ally and financier in uprisings against the Habsburgs. The ideas of the French Revolution were adapted to local conditions. "Liberty" meant the nobles' own freedom as defined by the constitution, "equality" meant the equality of all nobles, and "fraternity" meant being prepared to cooperate with nobles of a different religious persuasion. They had no intention of extending notions of fraternity and equality to include the non-aristocratic. *Liberté, fraternité, égalité* – but strictly for their own circle.

It was usual for the aristocrats of Transylvania and Hungary to attend Western European universities. They went on trips to France, England and the Netherlands, and since they were subjected to fewer controls at international borders they smuggled Western literature back with them into the Habsburg

Baron János Kemény, writer, pastor (1903–1971). Courtesy of Petőfi Museum of Literature, Budapest

Empire. Sámuel Teleki's wife, Zsuzsanna Bethlen, built up an extensive book collection of her own. Miklós Bánffy at Bonchida and László Toldalaghi in Koronka were the last owners of large private libraries in Transylvania. Between the wars Baron János Kemény was the publisher of the literary magazine *Erdélyi Helikon*, with Miklós Bánffy as its editor-in-chief. Kemény made his castle in Marosvécs available for an annual gathering of Transylvanian writers. The beautiful Baroness Carola Bornemissza was a muse to them all, and indeed to the Zsigmond Kemény Association in Marosvásárhely, named after a writer, thinker and relative of János Kemény. Carola cooked for the writers and noted down her Transylvanian dishes in an exercise book (published as a cookery book in 1998). She was immortalised by both János Kemény and Miklós Bánffy in their written works. Bánffy had a barely concealed relationship with her for decades – before, during and after her marriage to Elemér Bornemissza.

In front of the bookcases in the Teleki Téka are low display cases with special editions from the collection. I walk past with my hands clasped at my back and look serious, as if I knew all about them. At each glass case I lean forward for a moment. The oldest exhibit in the library is Galeottus Martius' *Liber de homine*, printed in Bologna in about 1475. Sámuel Teleki's bookplate is on show too, with the family coat of arms stamped in gold and his motto *deus providebit*. One display case contains several volumes of Blaeu's *Atlas Maior*, brought from Amsterdam in 1689 by typographer Nicolaus Kis (known in Hungary as Miklós Tótfalusi Kis).

After I've been round, my guide tells me they also have rare prints from Plantijn in Antwerp and Elsevier in Leiden. On my way out I cast another glance at the dark arched corridor where three Teleki descendants lived in the 1950s like mice in a bottle.

PURDEYS, PLUS FOURS AND WHIST

Marosvásárhely, March 2009

Stefánia Betegh, a woman of blue blood, shows me around the house where she lives with her sister. This kind of elongated, low white house can be found in all the villages of the former Dual Monarchy. It lies in the centre of Marosvásárhely, close to the citadel, a modestly furnished place with several beautiful cupboards and tables. This is where they took in Gemma Teleki after she'd slept on top of a cupboard in the Teleki Téka and then lived in a cellar longer than any of the other aristocrats.

Stefánia: "I'm very attached to the old things. When I was six, irregular troops from Bessarabia, arriving in the wake of the Soviet Army, looted our house in Fugad. They loaded everything they could carry onto horse-drawn carts and they were planning to murder us. We were alone, just the women and children, and we hid behind the wine vats in the cellar while the pack marauded above us. I heard the heavy tread of boots. Mother put my youngest sister to her breast to keep her quiet, while the governess held her hands over the mouths of the other little ones. Father was taken away by the Russians. We hoped for years that we'd suddenly see him standing on the front steps, but he never came back. We don't know how or where he died.

"These two glasses come from our house in Fugad. We have two or three things from there. Our governess, Erzsébet Biró, worked for us without pay for another twenty years. She hid the case of silverware under a mound of potatoes in the cellar. That's why we still have a set of table silver, although incomplete. It's ridiculous, but my sister and I always use that cutlery, just the two of us. We eat with it every day, even if it's only a sandwich. We even use it to cook with. I cherish those few things from my childhood."

Stefánia stands straight as a rod and smiles modestly. "Ah, now you'll understand why possessions can lead to discord within families."

The older Transylvanians were strictly brought up. Seventy-one-year-old Stefánia Betegh told me that as a child she had to stand at the table during meals and open her mouth only when spoken to. After the communists took power, Stefánia worked in a factory from the age of fifteen, making tin cups, knives, forks and spoons. There were a lot of

Karola Szilvássy (Carola Bornemissza), late 1920s. Ráday Collection of the Calvinist Church, Budapest. Photo Róbert Szebeni Szabó

other children at home and they all had to live from what they could grow in the garden, which meant there was little to eat. As a result Stefánia became a fanatical sportswoman, so that she could go to canoeing camps where there was plenty of food.

Stefánia looks energetic and extremely fit. I've visited her a number of times in Marosvásárhely and I can't avoid the impression that the discipline she learnt at an early age helped her to endure deprivation later. Decadence and spoilt behaviour were not tolerated. Practically all the aristocrats I spoke to in Transylvania had had the benefit of such an upbringing, with its patriarchal simplicity.

Pista Pálffy, a friend in Budapest whose family is from Upper Hungary, told me he'd once heard his mother say that she didn't particularly care how he got on at school as long as he behaved like a true gentleman. "That was the idea behind the way I was raised; you were to behave correctly and to be a good person. My mother had a strict, principled upbringing." Her father was Count Albert Apponyi, the man who refused to sign the Treaty of Trianon and thereby became a Hungarian hero on a par with Winston Churchill. One time she took the train to Fót. She was too late to buy a ticket and no conductor came along, so she paid neither the fare nor a fine. When her father heard that, he made her go to the post office and buy stamps to the value of a train ticket to Fót, then bring them home and burn them. "My grandfather was a government minister at the time and he believed it was wrong to take money from the state. Can you imagine a minister in present-day Hungary or Romania doing a thing like that?"

Pista's mother told him there hadn't really been any writers who succeeded in properly describing their circle, by which she meant the titled nobility. The one exception was Tolstoy. He was born into it. The same goes for Miklós Bánffy, the Tolstoy of Transylvania. As well as being an aristocrat and the largest landowner in Transylvania, Bánffy was the author of a remarkable trilogy that focuses on the Transylvanian aristocracy. It was published in Hungarian before the Second World War.

His godchild (also called Miklós Bánffy) told me how the trilogy came to be written. A young author, Áron Tamási, had written a novel set in aristocratic circles and he gave it to Bánffy to read. Bánffy read the manuscript and handed it back with the words: "You're an ass, my son! You know nothing about us at all! I'll show you people."

In the second volume of Bánffy's trilogy the central character, Count Bálint Abády, relates what his grandfather told him about the family: "There is nothing at all marvellous or wonderful about it, my boy, and especially there is nothing to boast about. What has happened has been entirely natural. Long ago, when the country folk were all serfs, everything belonged to the landowner, the so-called noble who himself held it from the king. It was therefore nothing less than his bounden duty to take care of everything, to build what was needed and to repair what needed repairing. That our family have done this only shows that they have always done their duty, nothing else. Let this be a lesson to you!"

Grandfather Abády goes on: "That members of our family often obtained great positions in the state was no accident and no particular merit to them. Such places were naturally offered to people of high rank, nobles whose fortunes and family connections were necessary if they were to do a useful job. We can be proud that our forebears honestly carried out what was expected of them, that is all. Family conceit because of such things is not only ridiculous but also dangerous to the character of those who come to believe in it."

A few years ago I read a report in the Dutch daily newspaper *de Volkskrant* about Eton, the English boarding school for descendants of long-established families. I'm convinced it's because of its school system that Britain has so many eccentrics. When I was thirteen I spent a summer at a similar sort of school (Stowe) and I can still remember the dark corridors, the halls, the wide staircases, the grey stone, the follies on islands in the lake, the enormous playing fields, the private golf course, the draughty dormitories, the canteen with sausages and greasy eggs for breakfast, and I can imagine the influence all of that must have on a child's constitution. Sometimes I think the brain is little more than a camera obscura, with an image of the surrounding architecture on its projection screen.

Taking young children away from their parents and putting them in huge Victorian buildings surrounded by parkland and misty meadows, usually with other children of the same sex, and the stress on sports, that strange combination of competitiveness and intimacy — it must all make for a special kind of upbringing. A more distant, more formal relationship with the parents and the development of a phlegmatic character are almost inevitable.

The article about Eton included a list of former pupils and their current occupations. The school continues to produce ministers, explorers, writers, artists, directors, mountaineers, balloonists, ambassadors and the sort of men who walk across Afghanistan with a dog for company. I asked Pista Pálffy in his capacity as expert on the English upper classes — he spends half the year in England and the other half in Hungary — how such a school could calmly go on producing adventurers and eccentrics in this egalitarian age.

"It's very simple", he said. "At the average school you don't learn manners. You're put into a mould and taught how to think. At public schools like Eton you learn how to behave, you learn to feel at ease in a dinner suit and tails, you learn how to greet someone and how to get along with all kinds of different people, those formalities that seem so pointless. In short, although you learn manners you're left completely free in your thinking. That's why those schools produce students with true freedom of mind, whereas the state schools turn out people who think in the obligatory clichés: perfect bureaucrats."

In Hungary and Transylvania I have friends of my parents' or grandparents' age. Theirs is a witty, original, forthright way of speaking, with an elegance and spirit that belong to a different era. You can speak freely about anything. The older generation

Count Miklós Bánffy in 1936. Courtesy of Petőfi Museum of Literature, Budapest

seems to have a preference for the eccentric, just as the English commonly do. Their childhood, with distant parents, an army of strict governesses and tutors, and castles and palaces with long corridors and extensive grounds, had something of the atmosphere of an English public school.

Erzsébet T. showed me John Paget's *Hungary and Transylvania; with Remarks on Their Condition, Social, Political and Economical*. Paget, an Englishman, travelled through Transylvania in 1835–1836 and was received as a guest by the aristocrats. He was introduced to one of them and from there referred on from one castle to the next. Roughly the same happened to me, except that only a few of the mansions and palaces were still inhabited. The grandeur that revealed itself to Paget 175 years earlier seemed consigned to the past, yet the hospitality and the sense of finding yourself in one big family remains. I too was referred on from one to the next and received with tea, wine and dinners.

Paget fell in love with the writer Polixénia Wesselényi, widow of László Bánffy. He married her, absorbed himself in agriculture and viticulture, brought innovations with him from England and was admitted into the Transylvanian nobility in 1847. In the 1848 revolt he fought with the Hungarians against the Habsburgs. After the uprising was put down by the Habsburgs with the aid of the Tsar of Russia, John Paget fled to England with Polixénia and wrote, in exile, his *Hungary and Transylvania*. In 1855 he returned to the mansion in Aranyosgyéres, where he died in 1892.

John Paget describes the daily life of Transylvanian noblemen in the nineteenth century. Most landowners had large stables with ten or twenty horses. They hunted everything from partridges to wolves. If an aristocrat harboured an ambition to hold public office he could simply have himself appointed deputy governor of the province; if he chose to devote himself to agriculture, thousands of hectares of land were waiting for him, Paget says, and if he wanted to work for a good cause, then there was the peasantry, which depended on him for practically everything and looked up to him.

Paget describes the sense of isolation and how long it took to reach the nearest town, partly because of the poor state of the roads. In the past century and a half this has changed somewhat, but not a great deal. The distances are still considerable. One major difference is that the majority of the remaining aristocrats now live in cities, usually in Marosvásárhely or Kolozsvár. Generally speaking, only the young descendants live in the Transylvanian countryside, in old-fashioned isolation, having taken it upon themselves to renovate family properties recently returned to them, and to get them up and running again.

In the first half of the twentieth century the Transylvanian aristocracy felt strongly attracted by English culture. Aristocrats used English hunting rifles, bred English thoroughbreds, organised fox hunts, went about in plus fours and tweed, had their suits made on Savile Row, played whist and later bridge, even in a few cases studied in Cambridge or London, or married Englishwomen. When Hitler came to power in the 1930s, most Transylvanian nobles sided with the British, partly because they were repelled by the proletarian cast of Hitler and his cohorts. Weren't most Nazis sweaty boors in tight uniforms? Many aristocrats favoured the allies and opposed any alliance with the Germans; some, including Prime Minister Bethlen, repeatedly expressed this view in the Hungarian parliament.

In his memoirs Miklós Bánffy explains how in Hungary between the wars the influence of the aristocracy, which was generally in favour of reinstating the monarchy, declined under the Horthy regime while the Hungarian gentry, by which he means lesser nobles, gained in influence: "It must be said that the gentry as a class were far more reactionary and opposed to any form of modernisation than the aristocrats had ever been. One can say many things detrimental to the Hungarian aristocracy, but it was certain that they never lost their international outlook."

Patrick Leigh Fermor crossed Transylvania on foot in 1933–1934 on his way to Istanbul, and in the neighbouring region of Moldavia he fell in love with a Wallachian princess. In his introduction to Miklós Bánffy's Transylvania trilogy he writes: "The grand world [Bánffy] describes was Edwardian *Mitteleuropa*. The men, however myopic, threw away their spectacles and fixed in monocles. They were the fashionable swells of Spy and late Du Maurier cartoons, and the wives and favourites must have sat for Boldini and Helleu. Life in the capital was a sequence of parties, balls and race-meetings, and, in the country, of *grandes battues*, where the guns were all Purdeys. Gossip, cigar-smoke and Anglophilia floated in the air; there were cliques where Monet, d'Annunzio and Rilke were appraised; hundreds of acres of forest were nightly lost at *chemin de fer*; at daybreak lovers stole away from tousled four-posters through secret doors, and duels were fought, as they still were when I was there. The part played by politics suggests Trollope or Disraeli. The plains beyond flicker with mirages and wild horses, ragged processions of storks migrate across the sky; and even if the woods are full of bears, wolves, caverns, waterfalls, buffalos and wild lilac – the country scenes in Transylvania, oddly enough, remind me of Hardy."

FORBIDDEN LOVE

Marosvásárhely, 2009

Erzsébet T. admired Carola Bornemissza, Miklós Bánffy's lover, for being such a proud and forthright woman. She tells me that Carola's mother was a Transylvanian countess, but her grandmother came from Hochstadt, where the winegrowers lived, so she was partly of peasant stock. To Erzsébet this explains why Carola was such a strong, brave woman who made other women jealous. She was no hypocrite, never making a secret of her lovers. According to Erzsébet there were two: Miklós Bánffy, the former Hungarian foreign minister, and István Bethlen, the former Hungarian Prime Minister. In her salon she had large portraits of both of them in oils, Bethlen on one wall, Bánffy on another.

In Marosvásárhely I meet Emma P., who knew both Miklós Bánffy and Carola Bornemissza. Emma welcomes me in the corner flat of a residential block of unmistakably communist vintage. The place is full of boxes and reams of paper. Threadbare shawls and tablecloths lie everywhere. Emma is descended from the old Transylvanian nobility. She studied chemistry and at eighty-four she still has an extremely sharp mind, but as soon as I walk into her apartment it's clear to me that she has to get by on very little money.

Emma was born in 1925 in Kolozsvár. She knew Miklós Bánffy in the 1940s, when he was approaching seventy. Baroness Carola Bornemissza was younger than Bánffy. The friendship between Emma and Carola néni ("aunt Carola") was intense, despite their great difference in age. Carola was a great beauty, and she liked to surround herself with eccentrics and artists. For a long time she had a maid whose former lover was a murderer who had been executed. The maid lived in Carola's house, along with her child by the hanged man. A century ago, Carola travelled across South Africa by train, boat and donkey, to erect a gravestone for

Bánffy and his daughter Katalin in Bonchida, late 1930s. Collection of the Calvinist Church of Kolozsvár (Cluj), Romania.

a cousin who had fought in the Boer War and died in battle. Carola's marriage to Baron Elemér Bornemissza was not a success. They had a child who died young and from then on they lived apart.

Emma: "On 30 August 1940, the day the northern part of Transylvania was awarded to Hungary under the Treaty of Vienna, when practically all the Hungarians in Kolozsvár paraded through the streets in celebration, Carola néni came into the room crying and said: 'Transylvania is being split in two.' The rest of the Hungarian population in Transylvania was hysterical with joy, but Carola understood it meant disaster. She was extremely sensitive and intelligent, a really strong woman with a powerful personality that permeated the entire house. In the afternoons I often went to visit her. She would always be lying on the sofa with a violet rug and cushions that had a pattern of white lilies."

Emma produces a photograph album, oblong with a fabric cover. The pages are of faded black card, and the waferthin transparent sheets in between have a spider-web pattern. Emma slowly turns the album towards me. I carefully pick it up.

"That's her; that's Carola néni."

I'm a ladies' man. I may have seen a woman more beautiful than Carola néni, Baroness Bornemissza, but I couldn't say where or when. On her head is a white nurse's cap. Her face is both powerful and melancholy, radiating a robust pride. The picture was taken during the First World War. "Carola néni was a volunteer at the front", says Emma. Of course. How could it be otherwise? A lady with a noble streak, who cares for wounded men, the sort of woman who knows no fear and makes you, as a man, instantly forget your own fear. I hold the album and look at Carola. She must be in her thirties. What a superb face, the dark eyes filled with a mixture of astonishment and wisdom.

Emma: "In the summer of 1940 we often went to Szamosfalva. Carola néni used to swim in the nude. The young women had reason to envy her; she still had a wonderful body. At that time she had a rule that one day a week she would eat only fruit, nothing else; she was modern in that. She was on the women's committee of the Protestant church and she often went to help János Kemény at his castle in Marosvécs, where all the writers came together in those days. She was the centrepoint of Transylvanian literary life. Her clothes were always elegant, always black and white. Since her son died she'd never worn any other colours. He died very young. She never had any more children after that and she lived apart from her husband. Carola néni died with the nuns in Kolozsvár. She didn't want to see anyone any longer, not even me."

Carola Bornemissza passed away in 1948, a year before the entire Transylvanian aristocracy was deported in a single night. She was buried at the Házsongárd cemetery in Kolozsvár. Miklós Bánffy covered her grave in red roses. In 1939 he married an actress from Budapest called Aranka Váradi-Weber; some of the older Hungarian ladies in Transylvania ask themselves to this day what he saw in Aranka.

"I was a child", Emma says, "but Miklós Bánffy always spoke to me as if I were an adult. He was the only person who did that. After my grandmother died he was the only one I could go to. He helped me. It was a difficult time. War brings tragedy. He was a good person, extremely clever and certainly not arrogant. He returned from Budapest to find that the Germans had looted his property. He came to Kolozsvár at the risk of his life to try to save his palace in the city and his country mansion, Bonchida. His actress wife refused to come with him."

Miklós Bánffy was a discreet man; in his memoirs he writes not a word about Carola Bornemissza.

FOR FOUR YEARS WE DID NOTHING BUT DANCE

Vác, February 2010

"One day a Frenchwoman arrived to be our governess. Jeanne. She was very pretty. All father's friends came to lunch and dinner, leaving their wives at home. One time Jeanne danced for them by the light of flaming torches at the edge of the fountain, scantily clad. That caused quite a fuss. She was sent back to Paris." Erzsébet goes on: "The other staff were from the village here or the surrounding district. They often belonged to families that had worked for us generation after generation. Village children would come to us when they were young to be trained as cooks, gardeners or grooms, depending where their aptitudes lay. We had a chapel at the house. The staff attended the morning services there on Sundays. The most faithful servants were buried at Dornafalva."

I'm hoping the sun will come out. The awful weather has lasted too long. At ninety-one Erzsébet still wants to go to her country cottage in Márianosztra as she does every year, in the hills not far from Vác. She's shaky. Her voice is thin and unsteady, and the skin is stretched tight on her scalp. Two weeks ago she had a heart attack. There's a woman doctor living in the apartment block who helps her. In the two months since I first visited her I've watched her grow more fragile. Erzsébet was not just a relative but a friend of Ilona's grandparents, although they were more than ten years older. Their friendship went back to the 1940s, when Ilona's grandparents lived in Kolozsvár for several years. They once stayed at Dornafalva, Erzsébet's family castle, for three or four days.

"Father was on first name terms with Ilona, your wife's grandmother", Erzsébet tells me. "In those days you only used the familiar form of 'you' if you were related; people were absolutely strict about that. Men could be on familiar terms with men, or women with women, but members of the opposite sex always addressed each other formally. Ilona was a beauty, tall, slender and blonde. And half of Kolozsvár was in love with your wife's grandfather.

"I visited your wife's grandmother later, too, in Leányfalu, over on the other side of the Danube. You can get there from here in no time by ferry and bus. But I saw

The Bánffy Castle in Bonchida today. A portal with an 18th century inscription. Photo Róbert Szebeni Szabó

them mainly in Kolozsvár in the 1940s, when Northern Transylvania was made part of Hungary. For the Hungarians it was a gift. There was a cheerful mood, every night a ball. For four years we did nothing but dance. The Hungarian word *mulatni* is derived from "to pass the time". If you say *mulatság*, you immediately think of gypsies, drink, and that's what it was like: wine, beautiful women and music. I was still young then."

The conversations I have with Erzsébet gradually go further back into the past, to her childhood in the interwar years, at the family castle in Transylvania. A happy childhood is a solid foundation. It's as if the self-confidence that comes from happiness in early years is impossible for any tyrant to knock out of you.

"I was born just before the Treaty of Trianon. According to the first land reform after Transylvania was made part of Romania, which became law in 1921, the Hungarians in Transylvania were allowed to own no more than 200 hectares of arable land. My mother was Countess Bethlen. She died very young, in 1922. When she married my father and came to live at Dornafalva she went to all the houses in the village with a thick notebook and knocked on all the doors, sat round the table with every family and interviewed them: How many people live here? How many children? How old are they? Which of them are doing well at school? Is anyone sick? How many chickens do you have? How much land? She noted everything down. Father didn't know what she was doing. She compiled an inventory that identified everyone who needed help, every child who should be encouraged to continue studying, where to find the seriously ill – all without saying a word. Weeks later, when she'd finished, she simply laid the notebook on father's desk, confident that he'd take action where necessary. And he did.

"As a child I wrote a lot. In the winters we were often snowed in for ages and I couldn't go out. My father managed the estate. He got up at six each morning to inspect everything and discuss it all. At harvest time and in the sowing season he'd be up at three. He was an ornithologist, too. We had the largest private collection of stuffed birds in Europe, around 10,000 of them. My father had learnt taxidermy. As an ornithologist and hunter he knew exactly how the birds behaved and how they moved, unlike many other taxidermists. The medal hanging on the wall over there was won by my father in 1937 with a brown bear that he shot in Máramaros. It was the largest bear in the whole of Europe that year."

I find it moving to hear a woman of ninety-one speak so lovingly and admiringly of her father, almost like a little girl showing off in the school playground. Her mother died when she was three. From then on, in a time when parents behaved formally towards their children, and when governesses, tutors and battalions of servants further increased the distance between parent and child, her father must have been affectionate and caring towards Erzsébet and her brother, who was a year older.

"We always wore old things. Only when there was a ball did everyone dress up. The ermine, the tiaras, diamonds and satin were brought out then, and all the ladies looked like princesses. But normally the aristocrats went around in their old clothes. The Transylvanian aristocracy has never liked to show off. Whenever my father had a new suit made, he would get one of the servants to wear it, to take the newness out of it, before he put it on.

"When the staff or the children were around, the adults never talked about money, debts, divorce or any juicy matters like that. A man, an aristocrat, never mentioned his mistresses, not even to his best friend. Not a word. At table they talked about books, travel, nature and what would best serve the children's development. We had a fixed daily rhythm: schoolwork from six or seven, breakfast at eight, more studies until twelve, lunch with the nanny. From the age of fourteen you were allowed to take lunch with the adults and from eighteen to dine with them, but you were to speak only when spoken to. Those were the rules with us, and I think with most aristocrats in Transylvania."

The children were forbidden to complain, whine, snitch, stare, or eavesdrop on other people's conversations – actually everything the Securitate would later specialise in.

The Castle of Bonchida today. The western front with the gate to the park. Photo Róbert Szebeni Szabó

Erzsébet: "We had governesses from Britain, Germany and France, and my brother and I had a tutor. He lived with us. He was a good teacher. You have to teach by showing children things, not just by talking to a class, that's dreadfully boring. Our tutor accompanied us on our trips abroad. We went skiing with him and horse riding, and along the way, as children of eight or nine, we heard all about the ancient Greeks. We lay on our stomachs in bathing suits on the banks of the Szamos while he drew the countries of Europe in front of us in the sand with a stick. He repeated it in the snow with his ski pole in the winter. We did four years of elementary school and four years of grammar school at home. Then I went to Budapest to study for my exams and my brother was sent to the Piarists in Kolozsvár."

Erzsébet tells me that in Transylvania the eldest son would inherit the castle with its contents and estate, while the daughters and younger sons were given a house in town or a smaller estate, as well as jewellery and investments. All the children received the same amount, in theory. An old lady I knew in Budapest said that in Hungary there was a system of primogeniture. Her father's eldest brother inherited the castle and the estates, whereas the youngest of the brothers received an allowance that was barely enough to buy drink and cigarettes. The sisters were expected to make a good catch. The second and third sons were able to build careers for themselves with the Hussars or in the Church, where they would become bishops. As a result, in Hungary the properties were not divided up, so they were larger.

Immediately before the Second World War there were still thirty-four aristocratic families in Transylvania. They were all interrelated, from a long way back. In *Between the Woods and the Water* Patrick Leigh Fermor quotes a Transylvanian aristocrat as saying that they intermarried more than the Ptolemaians and actually all ought to be insane. One countess, Claudia Rhédey, is the great-great-grandmother of the English queen, so practically all the present-day Transylvanian aristocracy, whichever way you turn, is related to the British royal family. Erzsébet is a seventh cousin of Queen Elizabeth II. According to Erzsébet the rule in Transylvania was that you must not marry a first cousin, but marriage to a second cousin was fine. Mihály Teleki is credited with saying that in Transylvania everyone is related to everyone else, and if you're not related then you have an affair.

Erzsébet says that children born out of wedlock were sent to other castles, where the family would make sure the child was given a good upbringing and perhaps a chance to study abroad. A girl grew up at Dornafalva who was the illegitimate daughter of one of the other aristocrats.

Erzsébet: "From the age of eighteen, girls were allowed to powder their noses and wear silk stockings and low-cut dresses. They were introduced into society accompanied by their mother or another relative. The boys were allowed to smoke from the age of eighteen, to run up debts and to wear the family's signet ring. Before 1920 it was out of the question for boys and girls to be seen together in public. There were secret rendezvous, usually in the church or at a museum. If children wanted to marry, they consulted their parents, who would settle the issue between themselves. The intended's ancestors were looked up in the *Almanach de Gotha* and their family's property in the land register." It was a stable world in which everyone knew his or her place.

Erzsébet is sitting in her armchair. As darkness falls her eyesight fades. She still has one good eye. I have to go. When I stand up, Erzsébet asks whether I know how to kiss someone's hand. She'll demonstrate.

Translation by Liz Waters

---

[1] Archaic Hungarian word for "library" – *eds.*

LUCIAN BOIA'S TRAPS OF HISTORY
Romanian Intellectual Elites Between 1930 and 1950

Ambrus Miskolczy

Intellectuals are in fashion. A quick glance on the Internet shows that in the 1990s the first large published compendia on intelligentsia appeared in France, while a few years ago the encyclopaedic *Thinkers, Philosophers, Intellectuals*[1] was published. After the turn of the millennium, a plethora of British and American works were written on the subject. In Hungary, Paul Johnson became fashionable. His book[2] ruthlessly dissected left-wing intellectuals from Tolstoy to Chomsky, while right-wing thinkers were largely spared his opprobrium. Chomsky meanwhile argued with a touch of classical reasoning that intellectuals are "a kind of secular priesthood" whose task is to "uphold the doctrinal truths of the society", and therefore "the population *should* be anti-intellectual in that respect, I think that's a most healthy reaction"[3].

Lucian Boia's latest book[4] was apparently the result of such a reaction. It is a masterpiece of its genre and the subject. It is to the author's credit that he saves his readers (and himself) from terminological gymnastics. For starters, he does not bother with defining who is an intellectual. And why would he, when he has one hundred and twenty academicians, journalists, university professors and writers to do it for him, intellectuals in Romania between 1930 and 1950, the topic of his book. During these two decades, these people witnessed and in many cases played a part in seven changes of regime. To quote the title, they often walked, fell, or were pushed into the traps of history. For most of them, it was impossible to come out the other side undamaged in body or mind.

Although I often fell asleep over Hayden White's *Metahistory,* I never felt the truth of the work's thesis as much as I did when reading Boia: namely, that the exact same story can be written in different genres and styles, with metaphors, metonymies and so on… The irony of the Romanian historian is quite extraordinary as he mixes comedy and tragedy in the same narrative, sometimes even in the same sentence. For example, anyone in Boia's place would have dwelled on the juicy instances of the private life of King Carol II of Romania, but our author does not even mention them. He gives us instead the generous protector of culture, the champion of youth over the conservatism of old academicians. Carol aligned himself with the same young intellectuals whom Iorga – the king's trusty old history teacher and historian of the nation – condemned as immoral and pornographic (moreover, he did so at the inaugural address of academician Lucian Blaga). But of course, Carol does not get off easily either. Although he was held to be a fervent reader by his contemporaries, he says nothing about his reading in his verbose memoirs, whereas he gushes enthusiasm about the movies he saw. Some of the writers – the best ones, who later became fervent champions of communism – sang his praise, often in comically sycophantic fashion.

But there are certain things that only those of us blessed with an excellent memory understand. For instance, the fact that while academicians duly lined up in support of the royal dictatorship, Radu R. Rosetti bravely said "no" to it at the public referendum held to gauge its support. (There were very few among the millions who did so; even abstention from the referendum counted as an audacious act.) This courageous gesture was in sharp contrast with Rosetti's nickname: Closetti. The great general and military historian, who was the director of the Library of the Academy, was famous for regularly checking the state of the institution's toilets. Anyone with first-hand experience in the Library before its renovation will understand why this was necessary. (In contrast to the toilets of the old Lenin Library in Moscow where the unpleasant smells were completely masked by the even more powerful and dense smoke within which shadows of Raskolnikov-like figures would appear as symbols of cultural opposition, the faces in the Bucharest library betrayed only a painful resignation in the face of the malodorous fumes.)

By touching on Carol, however, I break the chronological order of the book. But 1930 is a good dividing line. For a short period at least, the king's ascension to the throne hinted at a promising new era. Later the political parties would burn themselves out and the radical far right, the Legionary Movement[5], emerged as a serious political force by the time the king proclaimed his own dictatorship. He was in turn forced to abdicate in early September 1940, after Romania was divested of territory in Transylvania, Dobrogea, Bukovina and Bessarabia, and Antonescu and the Legion took power between January 1940 and 23 August 1944. This was the day when King Michael I – who succeeded his father back in September 1940 – arrested the "leader", and Romania turned against Hitler, not a turn of events hailed by the Soviets who had planned to march into Bucharest as glorious liberators. Three years of transient democracy followed, which was doomed to failure. In December 1947 King Michael was forced to abdicate, and a People's Republic was proclaimed. Communism, and its "dictatorship of the proletariat" period, had arrived. By 1950, the communist dictatorship was firmly established; and only a few internal political struggles remained to be fought.

Lucian Boia first sketches a collective portrait of the different intellectual groups. He begins with the "offensive of the young", those whom the thirty-year-old literary critic, George Călinescu called "puppies" in 1929, and who in turn thought that 30-year-olds were senile old farts. One of their representatives, Cioran, who spoke from their heart and in their name, opined from a distance of sixty years that the conflict between generations had nowhere been as fierce as in Romania in those days. The young communists and fascists got on quite well for some time, however. They appeared to believe that exchange of ideas was possible, until gradually, front-lines hardened by 1934.

Interestingly, it was thanks to the more nationalist and cosmopolitan members of this group, for example Mircea Eliade and Cioran, that "Romania at last joined the international choir". However, it was a university professor in his forties, Nae Ionescu, a philosopher and journalist, who really mesmerised the revolutionary youth. The impact and relevance of his oeuvre is still hotly debated even today. According to Boia, he is "a philosopher without an oeuvre", and his courses were "foggy". But his university classes had a mind-liberating effect. To illustrate what a lecture by Ionescu meant to his young audience, Boia quotes from one of his admirers' diaries: "He mocks systems and philosophies. It is a philosophy of facts. Everyone begins philosophising with him. Communion is possible, cooperation is not. [...] we come even with being, with ourselves. [...] There are no solutions. Philosophy has no use and does not help. Only we, ourselves alone, the creative process. The scholarly philosopher – he is a grocer selling someone else's cheese. [...] One must start from oneself, not from the other." Why would the "Professor" need a life-work? – asks Boia. His role was to open "forbidden doors". What Boia could have written about, however, is the Professor's political activity. After he became disillusioned with the king and emerged as the ideologue of the Legionary Movement – for which he was interned several times –, he finally offered to mediate between the monarch and the movement, but the king did not take him seriously. Unlike the Germans, who apparently did take him very seriously, judging from the fact that he lived in a luxury far above the average standard of living of a university professor – until he suddenly died of poisoning, conforming with legionary tradition. Nae Ionescu was a classic example of the intellectual gone astray, but was also a genius. The author understandably does not go into deep detail here for the sake of the book's conciseness and focus, the "gossipology" of Romanian history after all is inexhaustible.

The chapter entitled "Nationalists and Democrats, Jews and Anti-Semites" is an exquisite mixture of cultural history and public history, in which casual remarks alternate with harsh critiques. "Political disputes in Romania during the 1930s revolved around democracy and nationalism. The two could not be reconciled. For some, Romania was not democratic enough, for others, it was not Romanian enough. Everyone was right: either from the point of view of democratic philosophy or from that of the nation state."

Boia appeared to have been presenting the national landscape from a distance, but in the next sentence he takes a clear position: "In contrast, the communist regime made interwar Romania look more democratic than it actually was." The urban population represented only 20% of the total population, and the left was weak, due to the relatively small working class. Quoting the estimate of Liviu Rotman's monograph, the author states that in 1930, the membership of the communist party was 27% Hungarian, 23% Romanian, and 18% Jewish (unfortunately the author says nothing about the remaining 32%). But this is a "delicate" question, leading to a dangerous maze of assumptions. Boia simply cuts the Gordian knot (or what many think to be it): "It would have been difficult for a Romanian democrat to find his or her place in such a 'mongrel' democratic wing."

But the author had no intention of solving the problem of nationalism. He articulates a "politically correct" standpoint: "Today, democracy is good and nationalism is bad." Historically, Romanian nationalism is very deeply rooted. Romania declared itself to be a national state, but it was not, just like it was not multinational either; it was midway between the two, Boia says. In a kind of psychosis, the young nationalists thought that the dynamics of Romanian demography were less favourable than they were in reality. Eliade, for instance, lamented the fact that minorities were gaining ground. "It is irrelevant whether he was right or not; what is important is that he believed it", the author says. While others were living their own lives, Jews were at fault in wanting to become Romanianised or to acquire a double identity, and thus were active "in the heart of the community". (In 1936, the 24 year-old Cioran said: "Hungarians hate us from afar, Jews hate us from the centre, in our very midst. How could we, a poor people, assimilate the most irreducible phenomenon of history? How could a people who saw the light during the darkness of Hungarians, Turks and Greeks, assimilate another people, which boasts of having conquered the greatest peoples in history? The Jewish vitality is so aggressive and the Jewish acquisitiveness is so tenacious that our tolerance towards this arduous and exploiting people would certainly bring downfall on us.")

The 50-year-old liberal, the literary critic Eugen Lovinescu, also had "racist ideas", although "in a strictly intellectual sense". The Jews are the ferment of modernity – in the positive sense of the word. There can be no question of a "Semitic mentality", but there is undoubtedly a mental resilience. Their leftism is natural, they are over-represented in the left not only in Romania but worldwide. With extremist movements gaining popularity, this became even more emphasised. Jewish writers – or those who were thought to be ones – were driven out of the moderate right-wing press. Even Iorga, who broke with his pre-World War I anti-Semitism, sometimes reverted to his harsh old views although he mostly bothered himself with protecting the nation's morality from the pornographic poetry of Tudor Arghezi, who was hailed as the greatest poet of his time.

The leftist democratic press defended itself as best as it could, and leaned toward the communists. The major forum of democratic values engaged the legendary M. Sadoveanu, who, besides writing, was mostly interested in hunting, fishing and attending to his farm, according to Boia. "His ideological standpoint is somewhat unclear", and he defended himself rather awkwardly, Boia says. "It was quite difficult for Sadoveanu to be friends with both sides at the same time!" Ironically, it was M. Roller, considered by the secret police a communist, who stood up for freedom of conscience and opinion. "It seems they were not much mistaken", since Roller later became the theoretician of communist historiography. It is understandable that Boia did not miss that point, as historiography's "little dictator" was – according to eye and ear witnesses – a horrible person.

Interestingly, the author seems to be slightly more broad-minded with personalities who erred at some stage of their lives – and it is certainly true that a Mircea Eliade fares better here than Roller. Moreover, Eliade is out of favour these days. He deserves some leeway, Boia says, because for him, "legionarism meant love and freedom, elevation and intellectual purification". Apart from how we see things today – and they are always more complicated than they seem at first glance –, we should take into account not only the history we know, but also the one which Eliade "naïvely believed in", even when he was writing articles against the Jewish "conquerors". He was an anti-Semite, right, but less than others; and besides, he wrote articles in their favour too. (He wrote about Moses Gaster, and praised Jewish philologists, but – it should be noted – he did this during the royal dictatorship, when he had to atone for his past links with the Iron Guard.) No doubt, the nature of Eliade's anti-Semitism was not fundamentalist but "circumstantial", and at the end of his life, he felt the world could not understand him – not after Auschwitz. It was the manifestation of Eliade's "terrible naivety" – says Boia – when, as professor of the Chicago University, he let the following idea slip in a series of interviews entitled *Ordeal by Labyrinth* with unthinking awareness: "For the Aztecs, the meaning of human sacrifice lay in their belief that the victims fed and gave strength to the sun god and to the gods generally. For the SS, the annihilation of millions of people in the concentration camps also had a meaning, and even an eschatological one. They believed that they represented Good versus Evil. The same is true of the Japanese suicide pilot."[6] I wonder whether those who gave the command to carry out "Nacht und Nebel" and ordered the liquidation of concentration camps and their staff, also believed that?

The chapter "Professors and Academicians" is a bit more cheerful, and more serious at the same time. It is quite masculine in character (since there were hardly any female professors) and very Romanian (in the ethnical sense). Universities became mediums of Romanianisation. The author shows this with concrete figures, and also that the number of Jewish students was quite high whereas there were hardly any Jewish professors. He also specifies party affiliation or preference among the professors. The most interesting case is probably that of P. P. Panaitescu, who was at first a liberal then later a legionnaire. His 1935 monograph on the voivode Michael the Brave (1558–1601) does not mention national unity, and depicts the voivode as a mere representative of boyar interests. The nationalistic public, in particular Iorga, was duly outraged. The work's duality, scientific objectivity and political statement "could be" explained – in Boia's view – by ambition. But what could fuel this ambition Boia declines to tell us. Because while he notes that Panaitescu did not resort to legionary mysticism in explaining historical developments, he neglects to tell us that he did so amply in many of his articles. It would seem he revolted against international capitalism. He used a set of metaphors characteristic of fascism, and when he offered his services to the communists, he could say in earnest that the bourgeoisie was the common enemy. What neither he, nor his addressees admitted however, was that they all longed for the joys of this bourgeois existence, but in order to achieve them, they would have needed a revolution: a national one for some, or an anti-national one for others.

There were very few left-wingers at that time, but they would grow in number considerably. The person who dared to go farthest to the left was Iorgu Iordan, an excellent (although very boring) linguist and philologist who joined the International Association of Friends of the Soviet Union. He later admitted he had no clue of what communism really was about at the time. Boia bases his caricature of Iordan after Molière's *The Bourgeois Gentleman*, who had to learn from his language teacher that he had been speaking prose all his life: "Just like Monsieur Jourdain, who has been speaking prose without knowing it, Iorgu Iordan met communism without knowing it was communism he met." But to be charitable, the linguist professor, when looking back on those days in the middle of the 1970s, was most likely a little ashamed. Communism turned out to be quite different from what he bargained for…

In this chapter, A. C. Cuza, the grand master of anti-Semitism is without question the least favourably treated. At the age of 81, he became a member of the government preceding the royal dictatorship, a government that counted six academicians among its members. "He was very old and achieved very little" as an academician. When the anti-Semitic party leader was elected to the Academy instead of Lovinescu, a famous journalist even pointed out that Cuza passed "the exam in obscurantism".

The Romanian Academy was most sharply criticised by the great linguist, A. Rosetti, in 1936. He called its publications "a collection of folkloristic bogus papers", and although it counted the best philologists among its members, Romania remarkably still did not have a universally accepted orthography. (According to the academician S. Puşcariu, the orthography of certain colleagues reflected the state of affairs in politics.) Rosetti wanted a new Academy. "His dream came true. But apart from his own 'promotion', I wonder whether he was satisfied with the new institution", asks Boia rhetorically.

The next chapter centres on the king himself, and leads to the chapter on the legionnaires – just as the royal dictatorship was a prelude to the legionary rule. And a bloody prelude at that! "The two parties played a bloody game", says Boia. "Idealism and violence are the two inseparable faces of legionarism, which may seem deceptive: even today, some see only the project's 'purity', while others see only its criminal manifestations. Evidently, legionarism belonged to the great family of millenarianism, akin to ideologies that want to make a *tabula rasa* and create a new world (just like communism in its own way). It is superfluous to ask how it was possible that so many great minds were able to join the movement. 'Great minds' were attracted to it by its idealism, which, in its extremes, led to uncontrolled barbarism."

But King Carol II is more easily forgiven for committing the same atrocities as the Iron Guard, although his are equally "unpardonable slippings", explains Boia; "the state as such became criminal". In late November 1938, Carol had the leader of the movement, Corneliu Codreanu, assassinated with 13 of his associates (three of whom murdered the Prime Minister Ion G. Duca back in the last days of 1933, and ten others riddled the "traitor" Mihai Stelescu, with bullets, then cut him to pieces, for having smeared Codreanu). Then, after the legionnaires shot his favourite prime minister, Armand Călinescu, in September 1939, 252 imprisoned Iron Guard members were executed under the king's orders without a trial. Many of the intellectuals were relieved, in the left and in the moderate right as well. They largely fell into line, some even got uniforms. They later applauded Germany when it invaded France and when it forced to yield the king. The Iron Guardists took revenge: they butchered 60 imprisoned ministers, secretaries of state, prefects, etc. They even killed Nicolae Iorga, scandalising the public.

Intellectuals carried on getting even with one another. The purging at the universities proved an excellent opportunity: those newly fallen out of favour were expelled, whereas those without a doctorate could stay if they were looked on favourably by the movement, and they could wear their green shirts proudly. George Emil Palade, the only Romanian to be awarded the Nobel Prize, was almost fired from the School of Medicine in Bucharest under the pretext of lacking scientific achievements. Students denounced their teachers, among them Eugen

Coşeriu, later to become one of the most important linguists of our time. That was – in the words of Constantin Noica, a young philosopher – "the most beautiful madness", the reign of the Movement. Although it was put to an end in the next Romanian coup, conducted by Marshal Antonescu, many just turned their coats. "Pundits are easy to win over", Boia writes. But they were at least wise enough to remain silent then. Liviu Rebreanu, the greatest Romanian novelist, even welcomed the Marshal with enthusiasm in his diary as "a man of providence". "It is baffling and at the same time dispiriting how stupidly certain people can think!" according to Boia. But as the prospects for victory shifted, everyone changed. In April 1944 many university teachers turned to the *Conducător* as Antonescu was called, urging him to exit the war. No-one was hurt, says Boia, whereas before, people were relocated for expressing their opinion on far less important matters. There was freedom of opinion to some degree. In 1941, G. Călinescu published his monumental history of literature. Its re-edition in 1985 was a cultural event, applauded even today. It was not so after the first edition: for some it was too racist, for others, it was not racist enough. It was even banned for some time. No one recognised that the work was "a typical example of how not to write a history of literature", says Boia. It is unsystematic and ill-proportioned, and each chapter follows a different structure. Its tone is extremely personal, which is "either a great virtue, or a structural flaw". (Boia could have added that this magnum opus is an entertaining read, much like a family story written with malicious irony, in which the author criticises each family member except for Eminescu. Of course, while making a fool of others, he makes a fool of himself, too.)

The next chapter – "From one Dictatorship to Another… with a Pinch of Democracy" – depicts much jockeying for position. The wise guys stayed abroad, where many made careers and reached lofty summits, like Cioran, Eliade and Ionesco. Some even remained true to themselves and somehow got away with it, like the excellent doctor, Grigore T. Popa, the dean of the School of Medicine in Bucharest. He died indirectly from the character assassination he was subjected to in 1948 due to his consistent commitment to democracy. At the other end, we find Constantin Daicoviciu, an archaeologist, who was in turn a liberal, a Carlist, a legionnaire, an Antonescu fan, and in 1944, also a dean appointed by the communists. (One might add that at the end of his life, in the early 1970s, he turned against the theory of Daco-Romanian continuity, of which he himself had been a proponent. The quasi-religious official doctrine of Thracomania it seemed was too much even for him.)

Boia is right when, commenting on his own book, he says that the cases that impress us most are the ones that reveal the utmost steadiness or the utmost flexibility. In a way, they also amuse us. Ion Barbu, a hermetic poet and an excellent mathematician still respected today, was complaining during the exculpations that his career was hindered, which was true, due to his legionary anti-Semitism. But later he would often refer to his many friendships with certain Jewish mathematicians.

There is a famous anecdote here in connection with Călinescu: When Dej, the tyrannical party leader called upon the intellectuals to join the Party at a meeting, the literary critic replied: "The place of the intelligentsia is not with the Party – everybody froze at this moment, only to be relieved the next –, but in the Party!" Of course, this sounds funnier over a glass of wine, and it matters who says it and when…

Our high spirits are only spoiled by Mihail Sebastian's case. He was looking forward to the Soviet army and the revolution, but when they arrived, he found himself disgusted. "Should he have adapted to communism? – asks Boia. – It was not very plausible. For Sebastian, there was only one solution, prepared for him by fate: to exit the scene." The great playwright was hit by a car. In Boia's view, it was an accident, but the question lingers to this very day: who organised it?

Then we arrive at a snapshot of 1950. Exceptionally base figures invade the scene. Someone called Toma drags Arghezi's name through the mud, who refuses for a long time to collaborate, even when they offer him good money. Toma's father – a third-rate poetaster – gets a seat by Eminescu in the new pantheon. Călinescu has no choice: he praises him so fervently that the comrades begin to suspect him. He is observed and it turns out he tells nasty jokes. But since it was also common knowledge that Pavlov also slated Lenin, one of the shady characters within the upper echelons concedes: "we have to be flexible". Members of the humanities faculty are sacked; mathematicians, physicists and chemists are treated leniently, because these subjects "cannot be improvised", jests Boia. To avoid the risk of being embarrassed by them, outstanding humanities professors are subjected to gross injustices. In 1950, the sociologist Dimitrie Gusti, leader of the rural sociology movement, had his pension taken away; he was also forced to abandon his house leaving behind his library of 22,000 volumes. He was only allowed to take his bed, a table, three chairs and some clothes with him though, and in return he was given a room with no electricity and water closet in a slum. It was of course better than prison, and finally one of his communist disciples who got to the top, managed to get him a two-room flat. They also confiscated the estate and pension of academician and philosopher Rădulescu-Motru. He was given a modest position in the Institute of Psychology, where the almost 90-year-old researcher was encouraged to take his first steps towards Marxism. According to Boia, the only alternative was the Academy or prison; but we see that for some, a third option existed: destitution. Others were given high honours, like Cezar Petrescu, whom the Hungarian reader may remember – more fortunately – for his children's book, *Fram, the Polar Bear*.

It was the Carlists who found their way to the new world the most easily. The comicality of their flip-flop is alluded to by the author so subtly that those unfamiliar with the context might not get it. He describes Sadoveanu's book entitled *Mitrea Cocor's Journey to the Soviet Union*, as an "initiation journey of ideological purification" of a poor peasant, the initiation alluding to a freemason ceremony; Sadoveanu was a grand master and always professed that "the light arises in the East" *(ex oriente lux)*. One of his novels, *The Golden Bow* describes a Dacian man's journey to Byzantium also using the analogy of freemason initiation rites.

Lastly Boia notes that in the 1960s, even those who were sentenced to prison after 1956 gradually found some kind of birth. The state and its citizens "did not meet midway. The big compromises were made not by the regime, but by the intellectuals". Liberalisation meant that intellectuals could also become nationalists, and it is true that the chains were loosened. The often quoted "resistance through culture" was much more an "escape into culture". Communism recycled many people. "After 1989, no one was fired, neither university people nor academicians. They all went peacefully from communism to post-communism." There ends the "joyful" story, which teaches us that "some paid a lot for being consistent", while the choices of the luckier ones who were able to adapt usually met with success.

Hungarian historiography could learn a lot from the book, unlikely as it is to happen. Such a work would be almost unthinkable here. We conceal the affairs of our prophets with great embarrassment. And of course there is another thing we should not forget: the Holocaust. Even after 1990, a passage from Károly Kerényi's letter to Bence Szabolcsi, written in 1946 has not lost its power: "Unfortunately, in Hungary there are not only martyrs, but also many anti-martyrs, the new anti-Semites and those who take advantage of others' martyrdom, no matter which race they belong to. Because of these anti-martyrs, we have to think of the people at home as heroic souls of inconceivable patience, who no doubt 'left' again, if only internally. The deer[7] symbol did not lose its importance and significance for those who are people of the pure Spirit, in and outside of Hungary. That is why Béla Bartók is a symbolic figure for the whole humanist world, and I would regret it very much if you did not undertake writing that Swiss Bartók monograph."

But it is "embarrassing" not only what happened to the Jewish people, but what happened to those who were not or are not anti-Semitic citizens as well. Ferenc Herczeg wrote the following in his diary: "The whole work of revisionism, which went ahead with the consistence of a chemical process, was meant to reawaken the ancient sympathy civilised Western peoples felt towards Hungarians. And they sympathised with the Hungarian people because it was famous for being a freedom-loving, chivalrous people, already in the age of its forefathers. Well, I am not hesitant to say that our good reputation was destroyed by those wretched men who carried out the Novi Sad massacre and later the massacre of the Jews. A people that can tolerate its government to rob, strip and massacre thousands of defenceless people who were after all Hungarian citizens in the face of the law, cannot claim to be chivalrous and freedom-loving anymore. This is the disappointing truth that we must face, just like the fact that the Gellért Hill stands on the Buda side of the Danube." Engineers of the communist regime were also very cautious with the fate of Antal Szerb, Miklós Radnóti, Jenő Rejtő... and more than half a million other martyrs. Klaus Schickert, a Nazi and a Hungary expert, got confused when he thought the Hungarianness of Hungarian Jews was illusory: "When we cast our eyes across the borders of the Empire, Hungary immediately catches our sight as a country where the emancipation of the Jewry is without parallel, in its volume, power and depth. Hungary cast a shadow on all European states. How more difficult and painful the solution of the Jewish question will be here than in Germany!" Just like coping with the past... According to those who are equally familiar with Romania and Hungary – like Miklós Nagy-Talavera or Randolph L. Braham –, there are no Romanian Jews, only Jews in Romania, whereas there are Hungarian Jews. Therefore, the weight of the sin is also bigger.

Boia also writes about the two-faced politics of Antonescu, who liquidated the Bessarabian Jewry with exemplary cruelty and sly crookedness, but "only" had Old-Romanian and Southern Transylvanian Jews humiliated and robbed; he did not deliver them to Hitler. He makes fun of the Tomas and their ilk, writes with a healthy disgust about the Rollers, illustrates the anti-Semitism in the Party, and examines the so-called "over-representation" of Jews with figures. At the time he also mentions that many Jews did indeed hold high positions in the apparatus. I don't believe it was for anti-Semitic reasons that a few Jewish leaders were shelved at the beginning: when Dej came, however, with him came the hicks and cunning sneaks who did away with the intellectuals: the Hungarian polyglot, mathematician and physicist István Fóris, the intellectual boyar L. Pătrășcanu, the educated and more liberal Ana Pauker. Deceitful vulgarity won out over intellectual superiority.

Boia's presentation is very similar to that of the *Final Report*, which draws up the balance of communism. This is a unique collective enterprise; no such work was done in any other former communist state of Central and Eastern Europe. Its general editor is Vladimir Tismăneanu, who is only able to repeat I. Deutscher's "non-Jewish Jewish" paradigm, and to tell his own family stories. In the *Final Report*, communist "allogenic peoples (Bulgarians, Hungarians, Romanian Jews and Ukrainians)... understood the aspirations of the country and the people only to a limited extent", moreover, they were for the breaking-up of the "nation state". Boia speaks more openly, but when he writes about Jews, he does not have a definite opinion. But the way he writes about cultural functionaries is all the more pertinent: "they somehow ceased to be Jewish. They became abstract.

There is nothing particularly Jewish in their position. They are soldiers of the Party ideology and messengers of a new society and culture". They are clowns among clowns, or villains among villains – depending on how we see it and read it. Of course, there are many possible readings. The same is true of the Jewish writers whose tribulations are heartbreaking, whose writings on Jewish topics are interesting, but whose scribblings written in the service of the new world are nauseating and null, and there is only one way they can be interpreted.

It is no accident that the books of Lucian Boia read like novels. His authorial "ambidexterity" reminds one of Dostoevsky, who puts in place his – deeply unlikeable – characters by highlighting embarrassing moments of their lives. The author does not step above the historiographical landscape, because he was already put there by history. Someone who writes about the traps of history is usually prone to fall into them himself. Lucian Boia is an exception. His attitude protects him. His credo is the following: "I do not believe in the intellectual who makes politics, but I believe in the intellectual who judges politics, and not only that. The intellectual has to ensure the interplay of ideas and their free movement in society." Boia is somewhat like his youthful idol, the polymath Hasdeu, the great fabricator of myths who, to oppose the sterile science and historiographical boredom of his age, defined himself as a "non-doctor". Lucian Boia is a non-academic. But he occupies a distinguished place and not only in Romanian historiography.

Translation by Orsolya Németh

---

[1] Bennice, Warren G, *Dominant's Encyclopaedia of Movers and Shakers. Thinkers, Philosophers, Intellectuals*, 2004.

[2] *Intellectuals*, 1988.

[3] Mitchell, Peter R. – Schoeffel, John*, Understanding Power. The Indispensable Chomsky*, 2002, p. 96.

[4] Boia, Lucian, *Capcanele istoriei. Elita intelectuală românească între 1930 şi 1950*. Bucureşti, Humanitas, 2011. French translation: *Les Pièges de l'histoire. Les élites intellectuelles roumaines (1930–1950)*, Les Belles Lettres, Paris, 2013.

[5] The "Legion of the Archangel Michael", a nationalist, anti-Semite and anti-Hungarian movement, was founded in 1927 by Corneliu Codreanu. The "Iron Guard" was a paramilitary branch of the Legion, formed in 1930. (*Eds.*)

[6] Eliade, Mircea, *Ordeal by Labyrinth. Conversations with Claude-Henri Rocquet*, 1982, p. 126.

[7] The deer is a mythological psychopomp for the Hungarians.

WALLENBERG AND THE JEWISH DOCTORS

Tibor Pethő

"Stir up the embers of ire, / the flames of hatred! / The accusation falls on assassin "doctors" / who sowed cruel death – / let them reap the hatred of the people, / let them be swallowed by a bottomless depth / – those who would tear out Zhdanov's / faithful heart a thousand times…" – wrote poet Lajos Kónya in early-1953 in his poem reflecting on political events of the time.

The Hungarian general public first heard of Stalin's last great reprisal on 14 January 1953. *Pravda* published an editorial – allegedly drafted by the Soviet dictator himself – on doctors "on the payroll of imperialists" and in the service of Joint, a "Jewish bourgeois nationalist organisation". The piece was used in its entirety by *Szabad Nép* – the daily newspaper of the ruling Communist party of Hungary, the Hungarian Working People's Party. The "white-smocked assassins" – as they were called in the Soviet communiqué – supposedly murdered via mistreatment for instance Colonel General Shcherbakov, as well as Zhdanov, mentioned in Kónya's poem.

The editorial of *Szabad Nép* the following day insisted not only, as usual, that "the instigators of the bestial murderers are in Washington", but also that "serious conclusions are to be drawn by popular democratic countries including ours… that Joint's activities are much more widespread in Hungary than in the Soviet Union".

THE ZIONIST THREAT

The origins of the anti-Zionist campaign connected to Joint, a Jewish relief organisation, and the preparation of a large-scale anti-Semitic trial go back to 1948, and the launching of the fight against cosmopolitanism. The campaign in the Soviet Union then targeted "homeless cosmopolitans" of Jewish origin, primarily in the spheres of literature, music and theatre. (Ironically, a portrait of the 19th century German composer, Félix Mendelssohn-Bartholdy, who converted to Christianity, was also removed from the Moscow Conservatory.)

Hungary too launched its own anti-Zionist campaign in 1949, ironically lead by a cadre formerly attached to the Zionist movement, István Szirmai.

In the meantime, the Jewish Anti-fascist Committee, which consisted of Soviet Jewish citizens and which, according to Stalin, served only propagandistic purposes during the Second World War, was dissolved in 1948 in Moscow. One of its representatives, the actor Solomon Mikhoels, was murdered in what was made to look like a "traffic accident". All the other leaders without exception were arrested within a year. Their show trial was held in 1952; thirteen of the defendants were sentenced to death, among them Solomon Lozovsky, the former deputy to Foreign Minister Molotov.

The fight against cosmopolitanism was given further impetus by the Slánský trial, orchestrated in Moscow and conducted in Prague in autumn 1952. Rudolf Slánský, the General Secretary of the Czechoslovak Communist Party until his removal a year before, played an important role in the terror unfolding after 1948. Slánský tried to commit suicide in his prison cell twice, first by hanging himself, then by banging his head against a heater but was saved both times only to be executed "properly" by hanging.

JEWISH DOCTORS AND DEPORTATION

When in January 1953, the communiqués and incendiary editorials were published in the Soviet Union about the white-smocked terrorists on the payroll of Joint, many people, mostly Jewish doctors, had already been arrested. Yakov Rapoport, a Soviet doctor, was told by his interrogators right away that "you were arrested as a Jewish bourgeois nationalist and an enemy of the Soviet people. Tell us about the crimes you committed". Even if they only referred to it indirectly, the fabricators of the case left no doubt as to the fact that several functionaries from the highest circles had also been implicated in the "Jewish Doctors' Plot". In its first wave, 37 people were arrested, among them Jewish doctors working in the Kremlin. A letter of protest, written allegedly by renowned Jewish intellectuals, was drafted in advance. Finally it was discarded because it did not fit into the unfolding narrative of anti-Semitic propaganda. Doctor Lydia Timashuk who, according to the propaganda, "unmasked" the plotters, was awarded the Lenin medal (but it was revoked shortly after Stalin's death).

News about the "heinous crimes" of terrorist Jewish doctors and the exposure of an American spy nest shocked senior members of the party leadership. They were right in assuming that the Generalissimo wanted to remove them from power. At the 19th Party Congress held in autumn 1952 after a long break, many new men ascended to leadership who depended solely on the "Master". During the unfolding anti-Zionist and anti-Semitic campaign in February 1953, the future Prime Minister and always stylish Bulganin was so desperate to prove his innocence that he offered his help to Stalin in an eventual deportation of Soviet Jews to Siberia. (Even though he, unlike most of the Soviet leading elite – as the historian Miklós Kun points out – was not even an anti-Semite.)

It still has not been proved whether they ever actually wanted to deport Jews to Far-Eastern labour camps at the beginning of 1953. The son of Kremlin doctor Yakov Etinger – who was also implicated in the Zionist affair – recalls that from 1952 on, barracks were allegedly being built in the "Far-Eastern Jewish Autonomous Oblast of Birobidzhan", to accommodate deported Jews. According to Etinger, deportation would have begun in spring 1953 but it was put on hold due to Stalin's death.

ZIONIST PLOTTERS IN HUNGARY

Based then on the Soviet formula, Hungarian party leader Mátyás Rákosi gave orders to Gábor Péter, commander of the Hungarian secret police (State Protection Authority, or ÁVH) to prepare a series of large-scale trials at the end of 1952. The doctors' trial would have been accompanied by a Zionist spy trial. The previously mentioned Slánský affair in Czechoslovakia presented itself as a suitable model. The Czechoslovak secret police "confirmed" that Rudolf Slánský met with Ben Gurion on a secret conference where they agreed to establish an imperialist spy centre in Israel on US orders. In Hungary, they were looking for characters for a similar show trial.

In the meantime, the General Secretary changed his mind about the persons to be tried. Gábor Péter, who originally prepared the trial, suddenly found himself as a defendant. The ÁVH leader was arrested on 3 January 1953 in Rákosi's villa on Lóránt Street. Péter arrived shortly before from Szuhakálló, the site of a mine disaster where he personally tried to identify the "plotters" and 'diversionists'. (Even in the case of accidents, a culprit had to be found. According to the official Stalin doctrine, when the class struggle sharpens, members of the previous elite try to sabotage the socialist-communist regime more and more desperately. The permanent, almost war-like propaganda tried to prove the same – just as with the arrests, the military procedures and the executions for simply "sabotaging public supply". As a result, there was hardly any family which remained untouched by the repression.)

The concept underwent several changes and the list of "cosmopolitan Zionist plotters" slowly took shape. After Gábor Péter, his former and current Jewish colleagues were soon arrested, among others the Minister of Justice Gyula Décsi, law-enforcement colonel Gyula Princz from the Ministry of the Interior and Tibor Vajda, Head of the Investigation Department. (Tibor Vajda fled to the West during the 1956 revolution as a "freedom fighter" and settled in Australia. He worked there as a dentist, although he never attended medical school. One of his victims recognised him and he was consequently prosecuted. In the 1990s an employee at the Ministry of the Interior – and an ex-member of the ÁVH – wrote to the Australian authorities in Vajda's defence that "at the Investigation Department of the ÁVH it was not allowed to use torture or violence against suspects during the period in question, i.e. between 1950–52 . Head of department Tibor Vajda explicitly banned it." This was obviously a lie.)

István Szirmai, President of the Hungarian Radio, was also arrested at the beginning of 1953. About the same time, György Aczél, a communist functionary and future culture czar, who had been imprisoned since 1949, was separated from his cellmates, supposedly to be later implicated in the trial as a defendant alongside Szirmai. (Both Szirmai and Aczél were Jews and had both participated in the Zionist youth movement before the war. In Aczél's 1949 trial, Zionism was one of the charges.)

A day after the ominous *Szabad Nép* editorial was published, László Benedek, the former superintendent of the Jewish hospital and a leader of the Hungarian branch of Joint, and last but not least, a fervent communist, was arrested by the ÁVH along with a number of other Jewish doctors including the renowned professor István Székács, whose brother was in fact previously a member of the British intelligence under the code name Francis Shelton, although the two brothers were not in contact. One of the main protagonists of the Zionist spy trial would most likely have been a relative of Doctor Benedek, the party functionary and economist Zoltán Vas. He escaped arrest but was quickly removed from the party leadership and demoted to head of the Mining Trust in Komló.

WALLENBERG'S RESCUE ACTIONS

Raoul Wallenberg caught the attention of the secret police relatively early. Wallenberg, who as a Swedish diplomat saved many Jews in Hungary during 1944–45, was arrested by the Soviet Smersh ("Death to Spies") shortly after the Soviet occupation of Budapest, it is believed on 19 January 1945. The reasons for his disappearance remain a cause for speculation: was he to be an American spy, or was his kidnapping linked to his knowledge of the Katyn massacre by the Soviets in 1940, and to the fact that he secured some of the documents relating to it? (The equally mysterious disappearance of Zoltán Mikó early 1945, a staff captain who worked with Wallenberg, is also important. It was captain Mikó who, at Wallenberg's request, got hold of the Katyn documents. The Soviets wanted to destroy every witness and piece of evidence pertaining to the tragedy. Based on false evidence, Mikó was sentenced to death in Odessa by the Soviet army court in summer 1945 and was executed.)

In 1953, nothing precise could be known about the whereabouts of Wallenberg, and especially not in Hungary. The Soviet government announced a few years later that the late Swedish diplomat died in his Moscow prison cell in 1947 as a result of a heart attack. In response to the report of his death at the time, Deputy Minister of State Security Abakumov gave the following order to prison doctor Colonel Smoltsov: "Cremate the body without an autopsy." (However, something must have transpired even in Hungary: in 1949, presumably at the behest of the Soviets, the Wallenberg memorial – the work of sculptor Pál Pátzay – was hastily removed only a few days after it was erected.)

Raoul Wallenberg – who was sent to Hungary in July 1944 with American support partly to rescue people –, as well as Swedish journalist Valdemar Langlet, Swiss Consul Carl Lutz, and Italian businessman Giorgio Perlasca (who posed as Jorge Perlasca, the Spanish consul-general to Hungary) – just to mention a few important foreigners – saved the lives of tens of thousands of persecuted Jews, helped by their Hungarian assistants.

The first secretary of the Swedish embassy was in touch with leaders of the so-called Jewish Council – which was established after the German occupation on the Germans' order – on a daily basis. First with Samu Stern, and after Stern was forced to go into hiding, with Lajos Stöckler and Miksa Domonkos. He also met Pál Szalai, who was the police liaison for the Arrow Cross Party during the Szálasi regime, after the Soviets surrounded Budapest. Szalai had joined the extreme right Arrow Cross youth movement in the 1930s, an act for which he received a prison sentence. He later became disillusioned with the movement under Szálasi's leadership and left the party. He was reactivated after the German-assisted Arrow Cross coup d'état on 15–16 October 1944. By November, Szalai, who appeared in several newsreels at the time, had been appointed as the party's police liaison. He was one of the few Arrow Cross Party members who played an active role in rescue actions. Many people owed their lives to the young police liaison: he actively protected the office and the refugees of the Glasshouse on Vadász Street, led by Carl Lutz. It was also due to his courageous intervention that residents of the protected house on Üllői Street 2, among others Stöckler and his family, were brought back by Arrow Cross Party members from the execution site on the bank of the Danube. His most important deed is connected to the ghetto in Pest. After he learned that Arrow Cross leaders who remained in the city under siege were planning a pogrom, he quickly asked help from Wallenberg and Gerhard Schmidhuber SS supreme commander to prevent the burning down of the area and the massacre of the residents. The ghetto was saved and reached by Soviet troops shortly after. After the war, Szalai was one of the few acquitted by the People's Court – partly thanks to the testimonies of Lajos Stöckler and Miksa Domonkos.

WALLENBERG'S "ASSASSINS"

It was not long after the ghetto was saved that Raoul Wallenberg was taken prisoner by the Soviet authorities. The Soviet authorities still reassured the Swedish ambassador in Moscow on 16 January 1945 that the first secretary of the Swedish embassy in Budapest was found and "the Soviet military authorities will guarantee the protection of Mr Wallenberg and his belongings". But there would be no sign of Wallenberg whatsoever after that. Following Sweden's repeated requests, Soviet Deputy Foreign Minister Andrey Vyshinsky gave the following response: "After a thorough investigation it has been found that Wallenberg is not and has never been to the Soviet Union; his person is unknown to us… Wallenberg died during the Budapest operations or was captured by Szálasi's henchmen."

The Swedes did not believe the hollow explanation nor did they accept Wallenberg's mysterious disappearance. Thanks to further diplomatic communications from Sweden, Vyshinsky, now promoted to Foreign Minister, suggested in March 1952 that "the Ministry of State Security of the Soviet Union should see it expedient to revoke the opinion formulated by comrade Vyshinsky in his personal communication dated 18 August 1947". The Russians wanted to settle the affair of the former secretary of the Swedish embassy once and for all, and they thought it would come in handy if a show trial would prove that Wallenberg had been murdered in 1945.

The ÁVH probably cast former police liaison Pál Szalai in a key role in the trial dealing with Wallenberg's death. For instance, Szalai could have attested that the Swedish diplomat had been the Hungarian resident of an international imperialist spy organisation already at the time. (Another candidate for this "post" besides Wallenberg would have been Israel Gaynor Jacobson, former director of Joint in Hungary.) He could have attested to the murder of Wallenberg too, or could have been an accomplice as well along with his Arrow Cross associates.

Stalin's death on 5 March 1953 fundamentally changed the situation. Preparations of the anti-Zionist trial were aborted almost immediately in the Soviet Union. Some of the persons arrested were released saying that they had been victims of anti-party provocation.

The Zionist conspiracy was pigeon-holed in Hungary too. Gábor Péter was now accused of human smuggling, illegal issuing of passports and corruption, only to become six months later – following Beria's arrest in Moscow – the person most responsible for all unlawful actions, who deceived party leaders, tortured people and was accountable for countless deaths. The "case" of the Wallenberg murder now completely overshadowed the anti-Semite spy trial. According to the new concept, Wallenberg was killed in January 1945 not by the Arrow Cross, but by Jewish leaders. In the first version he was killed because he saved "too few" lives. This hollow story was soon thrown out at the ÁVH, to be replaced by the simple charge of murder and robbery. The "murderers" would have been former Zionist leaders who were originally defendants in the anti-Zionist trial: Miksa Domonkos, Lajos Stöckler and perhaps Dr László Benedek. Now Pál Szalai was forced to confess not that he participated in murdering Wallenberg, but that he had seen Wallenberg's body in January 1945 in the vault of the American Embassy on Liberty Square, then used by the Swedes. According to the testimony Miksa Domonkos, a member of the Jewish council was standing beside the body with a smoking gun in his hand, while Lajos Stöckler, who also worked in the Jewish council and later became president of the Jewish community in Budapest, stood on the other side. According to the new charges, Domonkos and Stöckler wanted to rob Wallenberg who was hiding huge amounts of Jewish wealth. The case was built on visceral anti-Semitism, using the cliché of the vicious, greedy Jew ready to kill even his benefactor for money. Szalai's former deputy at the police, Károly Szabó was also captured on the street as a possible witness. Szalai bravely resisted for a long time, Károly Szabó broke more easily – at least this is what the latter told Mária Ember in an interview published in *Magyar Nemzet* in the 1990s. But the prisoners eventually all gave up resistance under torture – which, apart from beating, consisted mainly of electric shock to the brain.

"Detective Szeiffert's method of investigation was mainly smacking. When he forced me to admit that I was an accomplice in Raoul Wallenberg's murder, I could count eighty-four smacks until I lost consciousness" – said Dr Benedek in his testimony prepared for his rehabilitation trial in 1956. There were other charges apart from Wallenberg's murder. According to a draft investigation report dating from the end of May 1953, Stöckler and his accomplices were also guilty of "delivering the poor Jewish population to the hands of the Germans and the Arrow Cross after their election to the Jewish council. When the ghetto was created, they practised favouritism. They packed all the poor Jews in a small place of inhuman circumstances, while rich Jews were given comfortable accommodation. They set up a web of informants after the ghetto was established. Informants reported those who opposed the anti-people activity of the Jewish Council [sic]. Those Jews who were reported were delivered to the Germans for forced labour, and many of them perished. They also delivered women to Arrow Cross men who then raped them. They carried out orders beyond measure, to the detriment of poor Jews".

RELEASE

Due to Rákosi's loss of importance and the strengthening of Imre Nagy's power, the political climate loosened and the trial was eventually cancelled. Stöckler and Benedek were convicted of minor infringements. The first man to be released was the completely broken Miksa Domonkos in the autumn of 1953. He was aggressively pulled from the prison hospital and placed in St Stephen's Hospital, where his relatives could visit him. His son, István Domonkos recalls that "we went to the hospital with my sister only to find our father in a terrible state. He used to be a strongly-built, athletic man weighing 220–240 pounds; now there was a wizened, crippled figure lying in the bed in a poor condition, almost beside himself due to the torturing. [...] We brought him home but we had neither the time, nor the energy to ask him about what had happened. In his present state we did not even want to try. After a few weeks he got a heart-attack and died. His death was clearly the result of the physical and mental torture he underwent in prison".

The thirty-nine year old Pál Szalai was freed in February 1954, grown old, with his hair turned white. At least that was how his former deputy, Károly Szabó recalled his old friend when he saw him by accident in the New York Café and tried to avoid him. Szabó himself sustained severe and permanent injuries during his imprisonment and died young in the 1960s. Szalai fled the country in December 1956 and settled in South America under the adopted name Paul Sterling, to avoid being recognised by his ex-Arrow Cross comrades. (But a book entitled *Hungarian Martyrs*, published by emigrant Arrow Cross in the 1960s still commemorated him as a national-socialist hero who protected the ghetto and lawfulness against extremists.) He visited Hungary again after the democratic changes, but was denied proper justice for his deeds back then, as he was deemed a member of an extremist organisation. After his death in 1994 he was honoured as Righteous among the Nations.

László Benedek, who was released in spring 1954 died in Sweden in the 1970s. Lajos Stöckler was freed in 1956 but died a few years later in Australia, suffering from mental health problems caused by his torture by the ÁVH.

The communists who had been arrested in the affair were also released from prison: the former president of the Hungarian Radio and first cultural head of the Kádár regime before György Aczél, István Szirmai, got out in 1954. Zoltán Vas was soon called back from Komló to the capital: he joined the politics of the new era, and became head of Prime Minister Imre Nagy's Information Office. Gábor Péter was sentenced twice: once in 1954 and again in 1957. After his release in 1959 he worked as a librarian. And finally, a few words about the arrested ÁVH officers: Gyula Décsi retired as a lexicographer of the Hungarian Academy of Sciences. Gyula Princz did not get party support after his release and worked as a bartender in a restaurant.

As for Raoul Wallenberg, even today, nothing certain is known about his fate, despite the fact that the Soviet leadership admitted at the end of the 1950s that he died in a Moscow prison in 1947. But even after his alleged death, he was still said to have been spotted by prisoners in different Soviet prisons in the 1950s and 1960s.

The poet Lajos Kónya cited above turned away from political poetry after the 1956 revolution; he died relatively young, at the age of fifty-seven in Budapest.

Translation by Orsolya Németh

THE TWO DOORS OF SÁNDOR SCHEIBER
The Scholar Rabbi Born A Hundred Years Ago[1]

Enikő Bollobás

ungary's Jewish history is rich in scholar rabbis. Perhaps the first was the Moravian-born Lipót Löw (1811–1875), erudite and dignified, and considered one of the greatest Hungarian orators of all times. As a proud Hungarian Jew, Löw broke with long tradition and gave his sermons in Hungarian. He wrote extensively on Jewish history, *Halachic* literature and Jewish education, among other topics, and also took part in both the 1848–49 Hungarian revolution and the struggle that led to the emancipation of Hungary's Jews in 1867. His first born son, Immanuel Löw (1854–1944), the revered rabbi of Szeged in southern Hungary – at that time a booming town with a thriving Jewish community – excelled not just as a scholar of Oriental languages and religions, but also as a botanist, with many publications gaining international recognition. Lajos Blau (1861–1936), the worldly director of the Budapest Rabbinical Seminary, professor of the Bible and the Talmud, as well as of Hebrew and Aramaic, was also a prolific scholar of Judaism, writing some 50 books and over 700 articles. The legendary rabbi of Budapest's Great Synagogue on Dohány utca (street), Simon Hevesi (1868–1943) was a historian of philosophy and religion (and of the philosophy of religion); his books on the enigmatic Job and the prophet Jeremiah, medieval Jewish philosophy and Kant are still relevant today, a hundred years after their first publication. The renowned rabbi of Nagyvárad (Oradea, Romania, today), Lipót Kecskeméti (1865–1936) was admired unanimously by Jews and non-Jews alike (among the latter, the language-proud poet Endre Ady), and was probably the most famous orator of his age, as well as a literary scholar and historian of religion. His brother, Ármin Kecskeméti (1874–1944), the beloved rabbi of the southern Hungarian town of Makó, was an outstanding literary scholar who also ventured into intellectual, social and economic history.

The list above of eminent scholar rabbis of the Neolog (Reform) wing of the Hungarian Jewish community culminates with one name, that of Sándor (Alexander) Scheiber (1913–1985), the ultimate scholar rabbi. He was everything his predecessors had been: erudite, dignified, revered, worldly, prolific, legendary, renowned, beloved. Hungarian and international Jewish scholarship has long recognised his unsurpassed achievements, while everybody who knew him personally was aware of his extraordinary humanity.[2] And also humility. Speaking on his 70th birthday to a crowd of several hundred gathered to celebrate him, he said he was "not a great scholar, just a lone survivor". And he added, "Those who were better than me either did not return [from the death camps] or else left us"[3]. Of course, this was incomprehensible to us in the audience – that anybody was or could be better than him – but the words weighed heavily upon our historical sense. He offered a particular perspective we had not considered before: the losses perpetuated by the Holocaust and communism, where the former decimated many of the best scholars, while the latter forced some highly trained rabbis to leave the country or abandon their Jewish identity by leaving the faith. I believe this was his intention too: to evoke our historical sense and give this joyous occasion a tragic, yet proper historical perspective.

Rabbi, scholar, teacher, Sándor Scheiber was the director of the Rabbinical Seminary (Jewish Theological Seminary) of Budapest – the only such school east of Paris, he was fond of saying – for over 30 years, from 1950 until his death in 1985 (in yearly rotation with Ernő Róth between 1950 and 1956). Here he received students from all over the Eastern Bloc, including the Soviet Union, and taught them Bible and Bible exegesis, Hebrew literature, Jewish folklore, as well as philology and bibliography. There were never too many students, seven or eight at most, so they could all study together in a one-room Jewish schoolhouse of sorts. Those who graduated became rabbis in communities all over the world – Moscow, Bern, Brooklyn, Sao Paolo, to name but a few.

I had the good fortune of meeting the man himself in 1967 in Cambridge, England, where he was researching the manuscripts of the Cairo Geniza in the University library and was staying with Alexander and Ibi Lax, a Hungarian Jewish family who had moved to England from Nyitra (Nitra, then Czechoslovakia, now Slovakia) in the 1930s. As it happened, I too had a room in their sprawling modernist house built in the style of Frank Lloyd Wright, and spent long weekends there during my time as a boarder in a local convent. Since the Lax's were extremely busy at the time, their most revered guest often had to make do with just me for company, a Catholic girl of 15. But somehow he did not mind. He sat with me for hours each night, telling fascinating stories about writers, scholars and scientists, making the lives of these intellectuals seem terribly attractive. And he was interested in everything I could speak about: my family, my readings, plans and dreams. Scheiber offered literary manuscripts for good answers to his many questions on Hungarian literature. And although I felt I knew nothing, I managed to "win" autograph texts by such Hungarian writers as Mór Jókai, Gyula Juhász and Mihály Babits. (Over the years I have come to treasure these gifts more for who gave them than for who wrote them.) And when his brother, Leopold (Titi) flew over from New York, we would all go to the Fitzwilliam Museum or punting down on the river Cam. In spite of the differences in age and religion, our friendship was instant, and lasted until his death.

Back in Budapest, this friendship embraced our families as well. Sándor and Lili Scheiber would come to our home for dinner, and then would invite my parents to their house. The meals may have been different but the thinking was very much alike. My father proudly recited the Hebrew prayers he picked up in the 1920s from his classmate Karcsi Héber – and another Jewish classmate, Paul Erdős – in Tavaszmező Grammar School. (Erdős of course would later go on to become an internationally celebrated mathematician – as well as my brother's mentor.)

Sándor Scheiber saying the Aleinu at the closing of Yom Kippur (Day of Atonement) services, 1983. Photo by András Villányi

I often went to the Rabbinical Seminary to visit Scheiber – *Sándor bácsi* ("Uncle Sándor") for me. He would take me around, again and again, telling me the history of the school, and about the tragic events that had taken place in the building in 1944. As we climbed the narrow winding stairs of the library, he would give long histories of the most valued books and manuscripts. They were still in a very sad state of disorder; it would take decades, he knew, to catalogue what was left of this once glorious collection, to store and restore it properly. I liked to sit in for the Bible classes of the professor – unanimously called *Főnök* ("Boss") by everyone else in the building – and listen to the lectures which he always gave without notes. (I was also learning Hebrew from István Berger, our beloved *Csuló*, so that I could attend the Hebrew literature classes too; but unfortunately my Hebrew never advanced very far.) And of course, I spent many long hours in Scheiber's office, filled with heavy furniture and valuable books (the irreplaceable ones were stored in the inner chamber, which I always looked on as a sanctuary of Jewish learning). He was never too busy to receive me or give me his precious time. Sometimes he would have other visitors in the room too; most often perhaps he would sit with his close friend, Samu Szemere, the Hungarian translator of Hegel and Spinoza; they did not seem to mind my presence, often including me in their conversations. Scheiber found many ways to make clear that he wanted me to visit him regularly. Once, when I was at university, I arrived home one evening, when my parents told me they had a surprise visitor in the afternoon: *Sándor bácsi* had dropped in, just to ask how I was doing. I phoned him right away; "If you cannot bring Mohammad to the mountain, bring the mountain to Mohammad", he said with an audible grin.

He had invited me many times to attend the services in the synagogue when one Friday night in 1968 I entered that sacred place for the first time in my life. I had never been in a synagogue before, and was so embarrassed that I just stood by the back wall, awed, hoping to remain invisible. But upon noticing me, Rabbi Scheiber got up in the middle of the service, came all the way to the back, took me by the arm and walked me to the first row. From that time on, I spent many Friday nights in this small synagogue, always staying for the *Kiddush* afterwards. This was a social event he introduced in the Seminary, the weekly *Oneg Shabbat* celebrations after the Friday night services. First the event took place in the ground floor cafeteria, later – when it became clear that the cafeteria could not accommodate the number of people wanting to attend – they were moved to the first floor upstairs, the great ceremonial hall of the Seminary, large enough to seat probably two hundred people and take in an additional one hundred standing. These informal gatherings served his commitment to connect people in two ways: they provided occasions for Jews, especially the young, to meet fellow Jews – to socialise *as* Jews – and they offered food for thought via the presentation of Jewish cultural topics. Scheiber would talk about a book recently published in Hungary or abroad; he would have visitors – the rabbi of Vienna or St Gallen, the professor of the Jewish Theological Seminary of New York or the first cellist of the Chicago Symphony – speak of their work.

He happily received visitors I took along whether they were Jewish or not. Among others, those who accompanied me were my favourite linguistics professors György Szépe and Ferenc Kiefer, as well as my brother's beloved mathematics professor from Moscow, Israel Gelfand. Professor Gelfand, then 60, spent his first ever foreign visit in Budapest in the early 1970s; since he was a most valuable asset for the Kremlin, he was guarded day and night by his two students lest he would emigrate. The two young men had been ordered not to leave him for a minute. They even shared the same hotel room for sleeping. Scheiber's Rabbinical Seminary was certainly a prohibited site for Gelfand; but since he and Scheiber really wanted to meet, we had to devise an elaborate plot (involving a serious heart condition my father supposedly diagnosed) to free him from the grip of his two watchdogs. We knew we were followed at all times, but were not stopped, and the two great minds did meet in the privacy of Scheiber's office. Later I also took along two well-known American poets who were visiting Hungary at the time to the *Oneg Shabbat* gatherings: Allen Ginsberg in 1980 and Jerome Rothenberg in 1982. Both read their poetry in English, while I read my Hungarian translations. Both were terrific performers, bringing the audience to tears with their poems on Jewish topics.

The atmosphere was always vibrant, verging on the chaotic, at least while food was being brought out and the meal was going on. People, happy to catch up with old acquaintances, were constantly on the move; small children, including my own (for after my two children were born, I took them along too), were crawling under the long tables. Food was always the same: challah with hot chocolate, the former broken into pieces and delivered personally to each guest by the rabbi himself (who sometimes, unable to approach every member of a large crowd, had to throw the pieces to the persons far away). He used these occasions for short but substantial private conversations, remembering every name, every grandparent's name, every problem the person was struggling with. What is more extraordinary: even in his public pronouncements he had a personal rapport with everyone; people had the feeling that his words were meant *for them only*. Like the rebbe in the Hasidic legend whose audience nearly gets into a fight when they cannot agree on who the Master was really speaking to: they all felt they were being directly and personally addressed. So this great hall was packed after Friday night services, for Seder dinners, after weddings and the inductions of rabbis. The synagogue nearly burst on Kol Nidre evenings with so many people trying to get inside. Above all else, Scheiber was a practising rabbi, the spiritual leader of his national community; and as such, he was responsible for all kinds of religious events, which he performed wholeheartedly and with the utmost personal attention. This is what he lived for: to bring people together, to revive the spirit and rekindle the flame of Judaism. He was a matchmaker on the grand scale, whose "matches" included not just marriages and lifelong friendships but recoveries of long-lost identities as well. He wanted every Jewish person to face the troubled past and embrace his or her often deeply buried heritage.

Indeed, as all reminiscences[4] concur, after the Second World War, Sándor Scheiber devoted his energies to reviving the spirit of Judaism in Budapest. He felt it was his duty to serve the surviving Jewish community, to rebuild the Rabbinical Seminary, to teach new generations of rabbis, and to pass on the tradition and thereby preserve it. "Refusing the most tempting offers I stayed at home", he explained in that 70th birthday speech. "What kept me here was my love of Hungarian language and literature. A sense of mission that it is my duty to help locate and preserve Judaica found here."[5] He knew that his task was, as later tributes put it, to "revive the spark under the ashes"[6], to "single-handedly revive Jewish learning and scholarship after the Second World War in Hungary"[7]. He became the man, indeed, who "built on the ruins", who would "heal the wounds of war and [would] bring a new renaissance to the institution"[8], the Rabbinical Seminary. Due to his tireless efforts, Hungary's Jewish culture did indeed survive under the ashes, to be later resuscitated after the collapse of communism in 1990. Were it not for Sándor Scheiber, who kept that flame burning despite constant surveillance and persecution by the communist authorities, there would probably not have been a Jewish culture to revive.

He would welcome visitors all day in his first floor office overlooking the Nagykörút, the busy *grand boulevard* of Pest. Somehow everybody was able to have his or her private time with him, when he had ears only for the visitor. Most often these were one-on-one private conversations; as suggested by the two stately armchairs: the room was set up for a meeting of two, a *tête-à-tête*. Given the flow of visitors, he had to set aside time for serious work elsewhere. So he left the Rabbinical Seminary at the latest 3:30, and by 4 p.m. he was settled in his comfortable study at home which was lined with books to the ceiling. He used a ladder with wheels to pick books off the top shelves. He still engaged in six to eight uninterrupted hours devoted only to scholarship, a time he used with relentless energy.

"Ein Leben ohne Arbeit ist ein früher Tod", he would insist. A life without work is an early death. He always urged his students to keep creating scholarly work. There was always so much to find, to uncover, to record, he would say. He was full of ideas which he generously gave away to others: ideas on topics, thematics, source material, critical literature, methodology – all to be worked out, drawn up. His recurring question whenever he saw me (or anyone else, I presume) was, "What are you working on?" For me he suggested several Jewish topics, some of which I took and wrote up into publications. One on the performativity of blessings in the Bible appeared in the Seminary's yearbook. In writing he demanded utmost precision; for precision was, he would say, the human equivalent of the divine capacity for truth. But he also believed that no truth was ever worth proclaiming if it hurt someone.

He was never pompous or sentimental. His sermons were always short, constrained, prudent.[9] There were no superfluous words in what were almost puritanical speeches; they were governed equally by compelling logic and impassioned yet unassuming poetry. Their power came from the concentration of ideas and the force of the argument – as well as the speaker's compassion and granite-strength convictions. And the general impression was, indeed, that he was speaking to each member of the audience directly and personally.

He had a tremendous sense of humour, ready with a new *Witz*, as we call these not always humorous parables in Hungary, for every occasion. I remember two vividly, since he told them often. Making a mockery of vanity and narcissism in general, the first one is about the famous dramatist, who, after talking about himself endlessly, turns to his friend, "Now, let's hear from you: how did you like my last play?" The other one makes fun of the Soviet understanding of philosemitism. It is about the conductor of the Moscow Symphony proudly proclaiming to the conductor of the New York Philharmonic that anti-Semitism is unknown in Moscow: "Out of the 16 woodwind players six are Jewish; four out of the 19 brass players, 12 out of the 32 string players" – and so on. "How is it with you in New York?" "Heaven knows", answers his New York counterpart, puzzled, not even understanding the question, let alone having an answer.

He was a man of contradictions. He radiated serene optimism and yet was of the deeply stricken: sombre, despairing, grieving even. He had reasons to be both: for on the one hand, he had a deep trust in the ever-victorious power of the mind, yet on the other, he was carrying the burdens of many deaths, including his own mother's, who died in his arms after being shot by an Arrow-Cross militia member. Also, he was saddened by not being able to bring more Jews back into the faith. "Judaism is not a proselytising religion", he would say half-joking; "I cannot even convert the Jews".

He was tormented by a dilemma that could not be solved while Hungary was still a Soviet-type dictatorship, even if a supposedly "soft" one. He wanted a more prosperous, more open, more vibrant Jewish community, which he knew would be in the interest of everyone. Yet he and his small community – like other religious leaders and communities – were under constant surveillance. The bureaucrats of the State Office for Church Affairs (*Állami Egyházügyi Hivatal*) – the arm of the Kádár administration policing and controlling religious institutions – were trying to keep him on a tight leash, harassing him and intimidating his students, regularly interrogating some and imprisoning others for alleged anti-communist and Zionist activities. The authorities were ready to crack down on anyone who they considered *too Jewish*. Jewish studies was not a recognised academic discipline; books with openly Jewish content could not be published. For example, for years Scheiber was telling Európa Publishing House they should publish Elie Wiesel; "he is a Nobel laureate in waiting", he would argue; but to no avail – Wiesel was also *too Jewish* for the Hungarian authorities, alas, and Scheiber died the year before the American writer received his Nobel Peace Prize. In this climate of official anti-Semitism, how could he persuade people to openly practice their Jewish heritage? His premature death was early in historical terms too: if only he had lived another five or six years, he could have seen communism crumble, making space for a Jewish community revival that he himself had worked so hard for.

There was another reason for his sombre disposition: while he was clearly the most prolific scholar of Judaism in Hungary, he was never offered a university chair nor given a proper academic recognition. Only in the very last years of his life was he invited to lecture at Eötvös Loránd University, Budapest; only at that late stage was an academic title bestowed upon him by the Hungarian Academy, an honorary position offered by Szeged University and an honorary degree from Debrecen University – all arranged by close friends, a fact that Scheiber was aware of. Even these recognitions came much too late; the harm had already been done. Yet he also knew that no matter how much the communist authorities might resent and punish him personally, his life's work had been accomplished: with or without the official stamp, Hebraica and Judaica had become established academic disciplines in Hungary. It was this accomplishment, this certainty of a *future in the past*, so to speak, that he considered his most lasting legacy.[10]

There was yet another reason for his heavy heart: he knew he would be unable to carry out the most important tasks he had set himself decades earlier. The *big book* would never be written. Instead, as he told his friend Rafael Patai, he "chopped up" his scholarly work and "dissipated" his ability on little things, small issues and minor details[11]. And dilution left no room, he thought, for the one comprehensive work. Of course, posterity has proved him wrong, for the supposedly little things, small issues and minor details amount to – as will be obvious from what comes below – a magnificent whole, a *grande oeuvre* indeed.

*

Sándor Scheiber was a world-renowned scholar of Judaism, with an unsurpassed and unsurpassable scholarly output. His honorary degrees (from the Baltimore Hebrew College, the Cincinnati Hebrew Union College and the Jewish Theological Seminary of New York) – although very prestigious – do not come close to properly measuring his accomplishments. For he was a historian of Jewish culture, a preserver of monuments, a folklorist, a Geniza scholar and a noted commentator of Hungarian literature, fields which all required a lifetime commitment. He spoke and wrote in Hungarian, Hebrew, German, English and French, and was not at a loss when having to give a talk in Italian either. He has over 50 voluminous books and over 1,650 scholarly articles to his name.

He believed it was in the interest of Jewish scholarship worldwide that the monuments, material and spiritual, of Hungarian Jewry be collected and published. Since the authorities would not allow such publications, he used donations from foreign Jewish sources to publish and thereby preserve these monuments. First he turned to tombstones in *Magyarországi zsidó feliratok a III. századtól 1686-ig* (published in English as *Jewish Inscriptions in Hungary from the 3rd Century to 1686*), and described altogether 154 inscriptions speaking of Jewish life in the Carpathian Basin between the 3rd century and 1686, the liberation of Buda from Turkish rule.[12] He gave detailed introductions to each, explaining how the earliest show the influence of Hellenised Roman culture, those dating from the Middle Ages bear the marks of Rhineland, Austrian and Bohemian-Moravian Jewish communities, while those from the era of Hungary's Turkish occupation show ties with German and Balkan Jewish culture. His archival research led to the identification of four old synagogues, two in Buda and two in Sopron. He gave detailed descriptions of the material testimonies of medieval Jewish life in Hungary.

Scheiber was also a preserver of the spiritual monuments. He searched archives of the region, identified 15 centres of Jewish "book culture", as he called them, in the Middle Ages. He discovered a new, formerly unrecognised place of Hebrew codices: in Hungarian book-bindings, where a whole new world of Central European palimpsest of cultures opened up for him. The result was a landmark publication, *Héber kódexmaradványok magyarországi kötéstáblákban. A középkori magyar zsidóság könyvkultúrája* [Fragments of Hebrew Codices in Hungarian Book Bindings – The Book Culture of Medieval Hungarian Jewry][13] still not published in English. He collected source materials of the utmost significance in the magisterial series *Magyar Zsidó Oklevéltár (Monumenta Hungariae Judaica)*, publishing in all 14 substantial volumes of primary documents. He managed to relaunch the yearbooks that had been banned in 1948, the year of the communist takeover, and from 1970 until his death, every year he brought out these collections of essays, memoirs, poems and other writings by Jews and non-Jews alike. He published several facsimile editions, among them, the *Codex Maimuni* and the *Kaufmann Haggadah*. Driven by his interest in Jewish manuscript illumination, he oversaw the publication of some otherwise unavailable Jewish texts: the spectacularly illustrated copy of Megillat Esther, as well as the beautiful facsimile editions of the Haggadah illustrator Asher Anshel, the calligrapher Lezer Ben Yeshaya and the book artist Marcus Donath.

In the mid-1980s, when a general thaw was spreading out over the Eastern bloc, the Hungarian authorities slowly began to give a green light to Scheiber to go ahead with the publication of some projects he had been pushing for. One such break-through event was the publication of the very sensitive diary – in Scheiber's private possession – of Ignác Goldziher, the world-renowned scholar of Islam. At

Sándor Scheiber in his private office in the Rabbinical Seminary, 1982. Photo by András Villányi

this time he also wrote several forewords and afterwords to books that brought Judaism to a wider audience, explaining and popularising Jewish traditions and customs. Scheiber's texts always lent authenticity and validity to their content. Examples include the album of the photo artist Tamás Féner on the various aspects of Jewish tradition and the posthumously published collection of cemetery photography done by Péter Wirth – both with Scheiber's afterword[14].

Scheiber was a bridgebuilder not only as a rabbi but as a scholar too: he brought ideas together. As a folklorist, he saw connections and parallels where other readers could only see dots, letters and pages. He identified Biblical motifs in literature, Jewish sources for phrases and proverbs, Old Testament origins of New Testament topoi, and the international connections of Hungarian tales and legends. Always paying "particular attention to concurrences between ways of thought and literature",[15] his interest was diverse: he traced folktale motifs back to Jewish customs, collected the names of Jewish musicians in 18th century Hungary, and identified Jewish motifs in Benjamin Franklin's *Autobiography*. In some cases his attention was microscopic, often following just one line or phrase back to its origins. In other cases his vision was macroscopic: he was taking it all in, so to speak, when, for example, he gave a full presentation of the Golem tale or the legend of the Wandering Jew as it appears in Hungarian literature. Three bulky volumes of *Folklór és tárgytörténet* [Folklore and Motif History] contain his most important Hungarian articles on folklore and motif history;[16] the essays written in English, French, German and Hebrew were collected in his *Essays on Jewish Folklore and Comparative Literature,* published in Budapest in 1985.

He was also a scholar in search of connections in his *Geniza Studies*[17], which he pursued tirelessly for 45 years and published ultimately in 1981. He was generally interested in Geniza: the tattered manuscripts which Jews, not permitted to throw away any documents that contained God's name, stored in the depositories of synagogues or buried in cemeteries. But Scheiber's particular interest focused on the scattered texts of the Cairo Geniza, and he pieced together fragments, some dating back to the 10th century, as he found them in various libraries of the world. He did most of his Geniza research in Budapest, studying the manuscripts collected by Dávid Kaufmann, the young scholar of the newly opened Rabbinical Seminary in Budapest in 1877. Kaufmann managed to purchase nearly 600 Hebrew, Aramaic and Arabic manuscripts and manuscript fragments of the Cairo Geniza right after it was excavated in 1896. After his death, his family donated the Kaufmann collection to the Hungarian Academy of Letters and Sciences, where it has been safely kept ever since. Following in the footsteps of such renowned scholars as Ignác Goldziher, Miksa Weisz and David Kaufmann himself, Scheiber deciphered and transcribed the various manuscripts and prints, catalogued and interpreted them. He then continued his systematic research in the libraries of Cambridge, Oxford, London, New York, Cincinnati and St Petersburg (then still Leningrad) to see what belonged where. He put together the missing pieces of hymns and poems and established the buried links in the private and official papers of Jewish communities all around the Mediterranean.

Due to his perseverance, prodigious memory and amazing eye for small details, he made important discoveries. For example, he identified a piece of handwriting by *remembering* – because Xerox machines were not in use at the time – the minutest details on three different documents which he had seen in Budapest, Cincinnati and Cambridge. He recognised that they had been written by the same hand: Obadiah, the Norman Proselyte from southern Italy in the 11th century. Moreover, among Obadiah's manuscripts, he found Hebrew music notes, the oldest Jewish melody found to date. Having put together the threads, Obadiah's music sheets were reunited after nine centuries, and the music came alive during the performances of the choir of the Rabbinical School, led by the conductor Emil Ádám, in 1972.

There was one discovery which he considered the crowning achievement of his life's work: in St Petersburg he found a signature which he authenticated as that of Maimonides, the Sephardic philosopher of the 12th century. For 800 years the signature was misidentified. Such were the thrills he lived for, thrills known only to a person of his learning and devotion.

Hungarian literature also belonged within his scholarly scope. His scholarship on Hungarian literature – which made up less than one-tenth of his total output – would in itself make him a recognised authority. Here too he was primarily interested in connections: how biblical or other Jewish motifs are used, often as if they were of Hungarian origin, by Hungarian writers. Scheiber wrote on a whole range of authors, among them Bálint Balassi, Mihály Csokonai Vitéz, Kálmán Mikszáth, József Kiss, Lajos Hatvany, Endre Ady, Jenő Heltai, Ferenc Karinthy, Ágnes Gergely to name just a few. But it was his beloved 19th century poet János Arany to whom he devoted most of his scholarly attention. "An idea that you cannot find in Arany is not worth having", he would say. He identified Yiddish humour in Arany, traced formerly unconnected lines of descent throughout the Arany *oeuvre*, showed connections between elements of Arany's narrative and those of Transylvanian stories, and offered convincing proofs to scholarship's dilemmas concerning authorship.

Scheiber, the scholar for whom gravestone inscriptions were of the utmost significance, chose a stanza from a poem by Arany to be inscribed on his own tombstone. This wish surprised some people; but for those who knew him, it was no surprise. Here are the eight lines from the famous poem "Széchenyi emlékezete" [Széchenyi remembered] as translated by John M. Ridland and Peter V. Czipott:

> He lives, who spends on millions the treasures of
>   His abundant life, although his days unwind;
> Still, when all earthliness is shaken off,
>   To a vital *principle* he is refined,
> Which will persist, and growing, grow more bright,
>   Though he himself departs in time and space;
> Posterity guides its virtue by his light:
>   As it desires and hopes, believes and prays.

Read as a tombstone inscription on this grave, it is the rabbi scholar who spent the treasures of his abundant life on others: Jews primarily. He will endure as a "principle", and a complex one too. First, given Scheiber's scholarly and religious commitment, it should be translated as Jewishness, Judaism, Jewish tradition or Jewish studies. But the fact that it is Arany's poem – originally written to honour the memory of the 19th century Hungarian statesman István Széchenyi – that is engraved on the tombstone of a 20th century Jewish priest adds another dimension to this idea. As if expanding the trope of prolepsis – because it places *future in the past* – the inscription celebrates the 20th century scholar rabbi in the words of a great 19th century poet, thereby interlocking the memory of János Arany and István Széchenyi together with the memory of Sándor Scheiber. So the "principle" gets expanded to encompass Jewish and non-Jewish thought and history, as well as statesmen, poets and rabbis. And future generations will measure themselves according to this principle as represented by Széchenyi, Arany and Scheiber, who are joined together in the great chain of being, where past and future meet.

*

His soul was joyously integrated; his faith in Judaism was not diminished by his commitment to Hungarian culture. On the contrary, he was a man who recognised hidden affinities and believed in building bridges. Determined to gather people and cultures of diverse roots, Sándor Scheiber always opened two doors: with one hand, the door of Judaism for non-Jews and with the other, the door of non-Jewishness for Jews, thereby making the point that the two are inclusive. While welcoming non-Jews in the Rabbinical Seminary, he sent his own students to institutions of Hungarian culture; while offering the accomplishments of Jewish culture to non-Jews, he conveyed the appreciation of Hungarian culture towards his Jewish students, friends and readers.

And he had blessings for both. In his address to the graduating student, when he blessed the new rabbi and conferred the Biblical blessing – *"The Lord bless you and keep you; the Lord make his face to shine upon you and be gracious to you; the Lord lift up his countenance upon you and give you peace"* – he never failed to include his own imperative, *"Be a Hungarian rabbi"*[18]. At the same time, he bestowed the blessing *"I bless those who bless you and I curse those who curse you"* on non-Jewish friends as well, protecting them from all future harm.

His openness towards non-Jewish Hungarians might explain why he spent so much care on his ever-growing manuscript collection. These were letters, notes, note cards and other papers written by famous Hungarian writers, scholars, politicians, painters and musicians – among them, Lajos Kossuth, Sándor Petőfi, Mihály Munkácsy, Endre Ady, Mihály Babits and Béla Bartók. Hungarian literature was a lived experience for him. That is why in his speech given at the wedding of his daughter, Mari, he cited one of the first Hungarian poems, written in Latin still, from the 14th century, from *The Legend of Saint Gellért*. Gellért (980–1046) was a Venetian priest, who became the first Hungarian bishop and martyr of Christianity. According to the legend written of his life, Gellért's philosophy rests on two pillars, work and art. This is what Rabbi Scheiber offered to the young Jewish couple to build their lives upon, the wisdom of an early Hungarian Christian.

In the fall of 1984 he spent his time at home, already too weak to go to his office. He told me to visit him often. My regular time was Tuesday mornings, and although I tried to keep these visits religiously, I had to skip some Tuesdays. At such times his wife Lili called, "Sanyi wants to see you, come over soon". One Tuesday morning, already in December, he phoned as I was just getting ready to leave, and told me to dress warm. He had a *plan*, he said mysteriously. When I rang their doorbell, he was already dressed, ready to go. He still did not tell me where, just gave me instructions to turn right here and left there. We entered the gate of the Kerepesi Cemetery, the national graveyard where famous historical figures are buried. This was not my first time with him in a cemetery, for he had often asked me to accompany him to funerals in Kozma utca Jewish Cemetery. But this time was different: this was neither a Jewish cemetery, nor a rabbinical function. He directed me to a particular spot, and told me to park the car. We got out. We were at the grave of János Arany.

It was a cold winter day, bright, piercing. Holding on to my arm, he wanted to spend some time at the grave of Arany. The two were engaged, I sensed, in an imagined dialogue under the famous oak tree planted there from Margaret Island – the great Hungarian poet in the grave and the great Hungarian rabbi on the bench. In the tradition of the kabbalists and the Hasidic rebbes, Scheiber was speaking with the dead; here with his beloved dead poet. I knew that I was witnessing a meeting between a "principle", as the Arany poem calls mortality transfigured into immortality, and a human being soon himself entering immortality and turning into a principle. I recalled a moment of similar gravity from July 1973, when we, a small group of friends, were celebrating Sándor Scheiber's 60th birthday in the synagogue. A fearful thunderstorm was raging outside, thumping the beat to Glinka's Mozart variations, the harp solo piece performed by my sister on the balcony. In that hour we all sensed that the elements outside the synagogue responded to our celebrations inside.

But at Arany's grave, Scheiber interrupted my musings of the human and the supernatural: he was ready to continue his cemetery visit. He walked me to the two grand mausoleums nearby, that of Lajos Kossuth and Ferenc Deák. Kossuth was the passionate revolutionary and later Governor-President of Hungary in 1849 (the revolution which, for the first time in Hungarian history, granted citizenship, equality and the franchise to Jews in 1849 by a decree which was to lose its validity after the revolution was crushed by Austria and Russia). Kossuth was a fierce defender of Jewish rights, who later famously denounced "anti-Semitic agitation" with these words: "as a man of the 19th century, I find it shameful; as a Hungarian, I deem it contemptible; as a patriot, I hold it blameworthy"[19]. Deák was the moderate politician who forged the historic Compromise (*Ausgleich*) between Austria and Hungary in 1867, which paved the way finally for Jewish emancipation in the same year.

We continued our walk to the graves of the widows of the generals executed in Arad in 1849, then on to other 19th century notables: the composer Ferenc Erkel, the minister of culture Ágoston Trefort, the sculptor János Fadrusz, the actress Mari Jászai, the family of the poet Petőfi. Sándor Scheiber said good-bye to each of them.

Finally, we found ourselves back at Arany's grave. We got into my car and I drove to his house in Kun utca. That was the last time he left his home.

[1] I am indebted to the Hungarian born American writer Charles Fenyvesi for his valuable comments on the text, especially for clarifying terms and concepts relating to Judaism. Special thanks are due to Alfréd Schőner, Rector of the Budapest University of Jewish Studies, for specifying historical facts and data relating to the Rabbinical Seminary.

[2] See, for example, the following collections of tributes: *Occident and Orient – A Tribute to the Memory of Alexander Scheiber*. Ed. Robert Dán. Budapest: Akadémiai Kiadó – Leiden: E. J. Brill, 1988; *Seven Tributes in Memory of Alexander Scheiber (1913-1985)*. Publ. Leopold Scheiber. New York, 1995; *A könyvek hídja – Emlékfüzér Scheiber Sándorról* [A Bridge of Books – A Garland of Reminiscences about Sándor Scheiber]. Ed. Péter Kertész. Budapest: Urbis Könyvkiadó, 2005 [2nd ed. 2013].

[3] „... én nem vagyok nagy tudós, csak egyedül maradtam. Akik nálam különbek voltak, nem jöttek vissza, vagy elhagytak." "Summa vitae". In: *Folklór és tárgytörténet* [Folklore and Motif History]. Vol. III. Budapest: MIOK, 1984. p. 585.

[4] See, for example, all the contributors (Moshe Carmilly-Weinberger, Curt Leviant, J. Paal, Raphael Patai, Hermann I. Schmelzer, Menahem Schmelzer, Joseph Schweitzer) of *Seven Tributes in Memory of Alexander Scheiber (1913-1985)*.

[5] „Sokszori és csillogó csábítással szemben itthon maradtam. Marasztalt a magyar nyelv és irodalom szeretete. Marasztalt a hivatástudat, hogy a helyben található anyag feldolgozása az egyetemes zsidó tudomány érdeke." p. 585.

[6] Moshe Carmilly-Weinberger, "The Last High Priest". In: *Seven Tributes in Memory of Alexander Scheiber (1913-1985)*. Publ. Leopold Scheiber. New York, 1995. pp. 1–5.

[7] Curt Leviant, "Alexander Scheiber". In: *Seven Tributes in Memory of Alexander Scheiber (1913-1985)*. Publ. Leopold Scheiber. New York, 1995. pp. 7–10.

[8] J. Paal, "The Man Who Built on the Ruins". In: *Seven Tributes in Memory of Alexander Scheiber (1913-1985)*. Publ. Leopold Scheiber. New York, 1995. pp. 11–13.

[9] His sermons and speeches given on religious occasions came out in one 400+ page volume, *Scheiber Sándor könyve – Válogatott beszédek* [The Book of Sándor Scheiber – Selected Sermons and Speeches]. New York – Budapest – Jeruzsálem, Múlt és Jövő Könyvek, 1994.

[10] See "Summa vitae", p. 586.

[11] Rafael Patai, "I Remember Sanyi". In: *Seven Tributes in Memory of Alexander Scheiber (1913–1985)*. Publ. Leopold Scheiber. New York, 1995. 15–17.

[12] *Magyarországi zsidó feliratok a III. századtól 1686-ig*. Budapest: MIOK, 1960; *Jewish Inscriptions in Hungary from the 3rd Century to 1686*. Budapest: Akadémiai Kiadó – Leiden: E. J. Brill, 1983.

[13] *Héber kódexmaradványok magyarországi kötéstáblákban – A középkori magyar zsidóság könyvkultúrája* [Fragments of Hebrew Codices in Hungarian Book Bindings – The Book Culture of Medieval Hungarian Jewry]. Budapest: MIOK, 1969.

[14] Féner Tamás – Scheiber Sándor, *"… és beszéld el fiadnak" – Zsidó hagyományok Magyarországon* ["… and tell it to your son" – Jewish Traditions in Hungary]. Budapest: Corvina, 1984; Wirth Péter – Scheiber Sándor – Jólesz László, *"Itt van elrejtve" – Tokaj-hegyaljai zsidó temetők* ["Here It is Hidden Away" – Jewish Cemeteries of the Tokaj Region]. Budapest: Európa Könyvkiadó, 1985.

[15] Alexander Scheiber, *Essays on Jewish Folklore and Comparative Literature*. Budapest: Akadémiai Kiadó, 1985. p. 15.

[16] *Folklór és tárgytörténet* [Folklore and Motif History]. Budapest: MIOK, 1977 (vols. I–II), 1984 (vol. III).

[17] See Alexander Scheiber, *Geniza Studies*. Hildesheim – New York: Georg Olms Verlag, 1981.

[18] "Légy magyar rabbi!" See, for example, the inauguration of Alfréd Schőner (1974) and István Zucker (1977). *Scheiber Sándor könyve – Válogatott beszédek* [The Book of Sándor Scheiber – Selected Sermons and Speeches], pp. 213, 215.

[19] "az antisemitikus agitatiót mint a XIX-ik század embere szégyellem; mint magyar restellem, mint hazafi kárhoztatom." *Kossuth Lajos iratai* [The documents of Lajos Kossuth]. Ed. Ferenc Kossuth. Vol. X. Budapest: Athenaeum, 1904. 117–118.

MAKING THE SILENT DEEP SPEAK
On the Danube-Concept of Thomas Kabdebo's *Novel Trilogy* Danubius Danubia

Norbert Haklik

> As I sat on the bottom step of the wharf,
> A melon-rind flowed by with the current;
> Wrapped in my fate I hardly heard the chatter
> Of the surface, while the deep was silent.
> As if my own heart had opened its gate:
> The Danube was turbulent, wise and great.

> *Attila József: By the Danube*[1]

"The fate of the Danube, flowing through the heart of Europe across Austria and Hungary in its watercourse that once was gouged, then stabilised and regulated, is to swallow up the discharge of its tributary streams so that eventually it swells to become the lower Danube. The fate of men and women living along its banks is frequently to be incarcerated between and beyond borders, also beyond Danube-borders, which is one of the most perverted things, except for the Dam[2] that is even worse than the border", Thomas Kabdebo highlights in one of his Danube-lectures.[3] This two-sentence statement quite tangibly points out the tension between the concept that depicts the Danube as a silver, sometimes blue waterway connecting nations, peoples, cultures and languages with the actual reality that sometimes is in harsh discordance with the idealised and desired Danube-picture. To present this complexity with the means of art is quite a daring endeavour, and doing so using the language-bound medium of literature is a particularly monstrous challenge.

Thomas Kabdebo's[4] *roman-fleuve Danubius Danubia*[5] takes on this challenge successfully, which makes it a unique work of contemporary Hungarian prose. The eight hundred page long novel trilogy, as István Tótfalusi rightly states in his review published in *World Literature Today*[6], is not only a *roman-fleuve* in the sense that the three novels constituting it add up to a "coherent story and recurrent characters, set within a not too limited frame of place and time", but also a *roman de fleuve*, "a novel featuring Europe's second-longest river as a main character". This in itself would suffice to qualify the trilogy as an outstanding achievement by an ambitious writer, but *Danubius Danubia* brings more than this to the table. The main stream of the trilogy's plot focuses on the life of 1956-er émigré József D. Szendrő (the letter "D" stands for Danubian), who after the fall of the revolution finds a new home in the small German town of Neuburg on the Danube, but embarks on a quest to reunite his family. This time plane of the work, ranging from the early fifties to the late eighties, in itself would provide ample material for a lengthy novel with its rich plot flavoured with political intrigues, murder attempts by communist secret police agents, Danube-travels accompanied by charming descriptions of nature, and a love story that never fails to maintain the involvement of the reader. But Kabdebo went far beyond these limits, as he tells a family saga of two centuries in the other time-planes of his work. The saga is told via a broad range of narrative devices that include diaries, memoires, letters and even a journey of the mind back into the 19th century that occurs only in the imagination of the main character, when he partially relives the life of one of his foremothers during a coma caused by a severe cranial injury. With the different branches of the Szendrő's family tree various nations take their place in the typically Central-European mosaic of the family. It is important to note though that actually none of the characters travels through the whole length of the river. Its entire distance stretching from the source in the Black Forest to its outlet into the Black Sea is fully covered only if we see the travels of three different generations as one journey, due to which eventually the plot of the novel itself constitutes a symbolic journey on the Danube. Hence the trilogy can also be interpreted as a virtual journey that redefines the river, creating a symbolic rendition of the geographical landscape, which presents the Danube basin as a cultural unity, from a perspective that emerges far above the national narratives, even though it is displayed via the life stories of individual characters appearing in the novel.

In this sense, the richness of the subject matter constitutes the severest challenge for the novelist who strives towards presenting the mosaic-like diversity of the Danube basin in such a way that it just strengthens the sense of the cultural-geographical-historical unity it all adds up to. The river that once used to be a long-standing frontier of the first typically multicultural European superpower, the Roman Empire, now passes through or touches the borders of ten different countries, is inhabited by people the religious diversity of which incorporates Catholicism, Protestantism, Orthodox Christianity and, at least in Hungary, and further on towards the east, has a significant historical heritage linked to Islam too. The river has an essential role in the culture, self-definition and folklore of the nations dwelling along its banks, but, not surprisingly, in ways that vary from land to land. The Danube appears in the national anthem of four Central European nations, not counting Austria, in the case of which it is not called by its name but, nonetheless as an obvious reference, is dubbed as "the river". Unity ends right at this point though, for the symbolic role of the stream differs from nation to nation: in the Hungarian anthem, alongside with its tributary Tisza it defines the geographical framework of the prosperity of the nation, meanwhile in the anthem of Croatia, being a symbol of Hungarian influence, it appears as a certain kind of an adversary of the country's other emblematic river, the Sava. In Bulgaria's national anthem the river plays a prominent role as a symbolic representation of the land's natural beauty, whereas in the Romanian anthem Andrei Mureşanu mentions the Danube in the more political context of the Russian expansion that threatens the integrity of an ideal homeland uniting all Romanians, by stating that "the Danube has been stolen". All in all, there is a vast complexity of national and regional narratives present alongside the Danube, and in the mosaic of the different truths along the river it appears to be an enormous challenge to accomplish what was described in the following way by Hungarian[7] poet Attila József in his poem quoted as the motto of this essay: "The great battle which our ancestors once fought / Resolves into peace through the memories, / And to settle at last our communal affairs / Remains our task and none too small it is."

Kabdebo's Danube trilogy does not ignore this diversity. The river not only provides a setting for the main hero József D. Szendrő's life, but all the crucial changes redirecting his fate are connected to the river in one way or another: it is one of the bridges over the Danube in Budapest where he manages to find his way out of the police car, throwing himself into the flow over the railing, it is a boat on the Danube in which he manages to escape to Austria, and even his death occurs on his own motorboat on his beloved river, just to mention the most crucial examples. One of his treasured plans is to row down to the Black Sea with his son György (nicknamed Gyuró), and in the prison cell he strengthens his soul by reading the diary of his father, describing a journey along the upper Danube. When in a letter sent to György he recalls his ethnographical studies at the university, he praises the approach of those professors who presented the Danube basin as a unity of higher significance than simply the sum of the individual countries alongside the river. He is also daydreaming about founding a museum that would present the entire ethnographic landscape of the Danube basin in a holistic way, emphasising the continuity in the folk customs of the various ethnicities that originate in the same source or that the different groups borrowed from one another. Kabdebo comments his hero's approach approvingly: "The Danube, as everyone can see or rather hear, speaks German, Hungarian, Czech, Serbian, Romanian, Bulgarian, also Russian and even Gipsy, and he, József Szendrő of the Danube, understands the mother tongue of the river."

It would be self-deceit yet to claim that József Szendrő's attitude prevails as a common approach in the Danube area. The novel brings numerous examples proving the contrary. To quote one expressive example, the uprising of Hungary against Austria in 1848–1849 "is a war of independence for the Hungarians, the defence of their empire for the Austrians, and the formation of their nation for the Romanians, Serbians and Croatians". The differences, and the frequently contradicting character of national narratives is depicted with the subtle irony that is so much a characteristic of Kabdebo's writing in the *Donau Tagen – Danube Days* chapter of the trilogy, which describes a Danube-conference ending up in complete chaos, due to the national sensitivities and the differences in the way the representatives of the various Danube countries tend to see their shared historical heritage.

The views of the individuals are, to more or less extent, inevitably biased (in extreme cases: fully determined) by their cultural and national background, and the characters of *Danubius Danubia* are hardly an exception. This circumstance must have led to one of the most challenging riddles Kabdebo had to solve when he was working on the concept of the novel trilogy, that is, the apparent conflict between the need to produce a narrative which works well as a "story" in the sense that its characters are flesh-and-blood human beings which the reader can easily relate to, and the novelist's mission he committed himself to presenting the events also from the perspective of the historical, geographical and cultural unity of the Danube basin. Kabdebo found a brilliantly inventive solution to this challenge, by introducing a unique version of the omniscient narrator (which, as George Gömöri points out in his review[8], is a "dying species" in our contemporary prose): the Secret Chronicle Writer. This narrator is timeless, unbiased, neutral, and, being the representative of the *genius loci*, the spirit of the place, sees the events form a much more elevated perspective than that of the individuals, or even nations. Accordingly, the Secret Chronicle Writer sees the entire Danube basin as one unity in regard of its historical continuity, and its synchronous diversity as well. To quote Kabdebo's description of this omniscient storyteller: "The Secret Chronicle Writer hiding in the beech crucifix acknowledged all this with satisfaction. He (and the Good Lord above) found equally likeable the believers of any of the religions in the Danubian lands (*horribile dictu*: including even the agnostics), the citizens of any of its states, and its frogs and crickets croaking and chirping in any of its languages and dialects. His suspicion was that humans are not searching for heaven's justice but for their own truth on earth, and they do not want to be heroes but survivors instead. The memory of the Secret Chronicle Writer, the nostalgia of the molecules making up the landscape recalled the times of *Pax Romana*, allowing him to believe that the obligatory concordance and make-believe harmony was once really the lifestyle of an era. Ever since feud, low tide, high tide, flood, rain, tempest, thunder, bloodshed and compromise ruled the life of most who dwelled here, even though they could have followed the example of the sunshine, that shone neutrally on all citizens starting from the hills of Schwarzwald to the fist-sized golden knob of the Saint Anna monastery's church that was built here on the mountain of Orsova."

Kabdebo's Danube trilogy can also be perceived as a symbolic journey on the river, the purpose of which is to express this unity constituted by the cultural landscape's diverse elements. In this sense the family saga of the *roman-fleuve* finds its visual equivalent in the mosaic mural constructed by one of the characters of the novel: Count Deggendorf. When depicting the tributary streams and the sights of the settlements along the Danube, the mural ignores the actual ratio of the objects and assigns their size according to their significance in the overall composition, similarly to the way Kabdebo is handpicking the events of history, apparently arbitrarily, but in fact based on their role played in the dramaturgy of the novel.

The most obvious proof for the trilogy also being both a symbolic Danube-journey, and also a means to outline the difficulties of seeing the Danube basin as a unity standing above nations, is the romance of József D. Szendrő's son, György Szendrő, and Annamaria Danubia Fischer-Galati (*aka* Bia), the story of which creates the backbone of the plot of the third instalment of the trilogy. It has symbolic importance that the two youngsters are participating together in an archaeological excavation, which repeatedly creates opportunities to express the connections and also the tensions between history as the creation of human narrative and current reality. Bia for instance, being Romanian with some ethnic Hungarian background, sees the contradiction between the Hungarian and Romanian historical narratives as a challenge: the way the teacher in the secondary school and the ethnic Hungarian grandmother from Transylvania are presenting the historical past would hardly have anything in common. Bia's solution is much in line with the eventual message of *Danubius Danubia* about the possible way of "settling our communal affairs": "It does not matter whether my Romanian ancestors have been living in Transylvania continuously or not, and it does not matter whether my Hungarian ancestors populated a deserted area or a rarely inhabited one. I will deal with other questions." The message in Bia's conclusion is obvious: it would be misleading to interpret our present exclusively alongside historical narratives. What is more, history fails not only when one attempts to use it to resolve contemporary issues of national-political character, but even as a means to settle debates of ethnic nature referring to ancient times. As one of the archaeologists points out to Bia and Gyuró: "On this level physical anthropology is the most untrustworthy clue. Even the Roman soldiers might not here come from Italy, but from Albania and Gallia alike, or any part of what once used to be Magna Graecia. Two skeletons can tell us about many things: the age of the buried, how long they have been in their graves, the physical condition they used to have in the moment of death, the quality of teeth, the varieties of dental illnesses, the presence, the lack or the frequency of the pregnancies of the woman, the wounds that the man got in battles or during fistfights. There is only one thing they cannot tell us: whether the buried one was Pannonian or Roman."

The moment when the romance of Bia and György finally gets fulfilled also represents an act of symbolic reunification of the male and female entities of the river. The key to understanding this is the scene when Bia and György are conducting the following conversation above the recently unearthed bones of the couple that used to live seventeen hundred years ago:

"Dominus danubius", said Gyuró.
"Domina danubia – domina danubiana", added the girl, varying it a bit.
"Homo, homini, danubius, danubiensis, pannonicus, mysicus", they kept trying the different versions, each of which narrowed and altered the meaning a bit more.
"Danubius, Danubia", pinpointed Bia.
Until now they were thinking about and looking at the skeletal people, and now, at each other.
Szendrő György de genere Danubiana put his arms strongly around the shoulders of Annamaria Fischer-Galati, alias Bia, turned her breast towards himself, then kissed her lips."

Danubius and Danubia, we shall note: these were the names the ancient Romans used to call the upper and lower sections of the river. Consequently the unification of the Hungarian–Romanian couple represents also the completion of the symbolic Danube that is constituted by the novel trilogy itself. It is important to note that in order to make the fulfilment of their love possible they both must break an oath that they had made long before their romance started. The injured Gyuró, waiting for his rescuers in a pit on Veranka Island, vowed to never ever cross the borders of his country, whereas Bia devoted herself to becoming a nun when she was worrying for the life of her father, who had been incarcerated by the Romanian dictatorship's secret police, the Securitate. To obtain happiness eventually together, they both have to detour from the course that life seemed to set them on in a moment of the past. The symbol of the romance is completed by the closing scene of the trilogy: when József D. Szendrő's life ends on his boat on the Danube near Bratislava, in the very same moment Bia's and Gyuró's first child is conceived near Nagymaros, and hereby also the symbolic Danube-journey of *Danubius Danubia* reaches its destination. The Romanian nation that inhabits the lowermost section of the river also finds its position in the ethnic mosaic of the family that lines up a long series of other Danubian nations – Germans, Slovaks, Hungarians – along its ancestors. This is the moment when the Szendrős become Danubians indeed – the family saga's stream reaches its outlet.

Thomas Kabdebo in his massive novel trilogy unmistakably suggests that the similarities and the common interests of the peoples and nations living in the Danube basin should outweigh their historical differences. Just like Bia and Gyuró, the Danubian nations also have to reassess the extent to which they allow their past to define their actions taken in the present, in order to accomplish a common, shared happy ending (even though this happy ending apparently must be preceded by grief). This seems to be the main message conveyed by Kabdebo's wholesome *fleuve-roman*, the novel trilogy *Danubius Danubia*, which is most probably the first Hungarian novel that keeps following the principles of the genre, and, by creating a consistent narrative, populates the realistically described river landscape with a multitude of characters that ranges from actual historical figures (such as Lajos Kossuth, István Széchenyi or Joseph Andrew Blackwell) to the imaginary, still quite typical everyday heroes trying to survive history on the banks of the Danube.

So it flows.

---

[1] Translation by John Székely. In: Attila József: *Poems*, London, The Danubia Book Co., 1966. Edited by Thomas Kabdebo.

[2] A reference to the controversial Gabčíkovo–Nagymaros Waterworks project, a large barrage project on the Danube that led to a still unresolved dispute between Slovakia and Hungary, after the latter had cancelled its participation in the project due to environmental concerns.

[3] Kabdebó Tamás: *Hármasság a* Danubius Danubiá*ban*. (Trinity in *Danubius Danubia*.) The shortened transcription of the author's lecture that he presented at the University of Miskolc, Hungary on 22 September 1998. In: *Új Holnap*, January 1999.

[4] The author, who left Hungary after the revolution of 1956 and now lives in Ireland, publishes his works in Hungarian as Kabdebó Tamás and his works written in English under the name Thomas Kabdebo.

[5] Kabdebó Tamás: *Danubius Danubia. Folyamregény,* Argumentum Kiadó, 2001, 2nd edition. The quotations from the novel trilogy appearing in these essay are translated by myself. N. H.

[6] István Tótfalusi: *Tamás Kabdebó: Danubius Danubia*. In: *World Literature Today*, Winter 2000.

[7] To highlight his view on his own Hungarianness more accurately, let us quote another section of Attila József's poem: "My mother was Cumanian, my father / Half-Szekler, half-Rumanian or whole."

[8] George Gömöri: "Tamás Kabdebó. Árapály – Pezsdülés". In: *World Literature Today*, Autumn 1996.

NOTES AND POEMS ABOUT RADIO

Igor Pomerantsev

THE AGE OF RADIO

It was the sinking of the Titanic in April 1912 that made the world fully aware of the vital necessity, the deadly seriousness of radio. The survivors owed their lives to radio; those who perished drowned only because of confusion in the ship's radio room and a lack of clear procedures for radio contact in a disaster.

Most listeners use radio as a source of information. But what kind of information? And how does it differ from what you find in newspapers or on television? It is my belief that the true, or as philosophers would say, the existential meaning of radio is in the magic of the voice, the magic of sound. And in this sense poetry and radio share the same element – air. My own personal approach to radio is as a sequence of sounds. They, the sounds, may be words, but not necessarily so. Drama, dramatic effect is created in the air, when sounds collide, smack each other round the head, rub noses.

My long years of work in radio are years of radio solitude. Editing tape is the work of a loner, an artisan, the work of a medieval craftsman: you do everything yourself, with your hands and throat, like a glass-blower. You are one-to-one with the microphone as well. It's scary imagining listeners, and I try not to. I think I am a claustrophiliac: I love enclosed space and being alone. I'm also scared of letters from listeners. I am convinced that, as they sit by the radio, many listeners are on a voyage round the world, no, into outer space more like. I, too, am a travel maniac: I jump from wave to wave, and then from wave to wave. I get a special kick out of working with archive material. Occasionally I get to re-edit – or cut, to be exact – the voices of dead Radio Liberty colleagues: the poet Georgi Adamovich, the writer Gaito Gazdanov, the theologian Aleksandr Shmeman. Then it feels like I'm working in a radio graveyard. All these people are dead now and radio is their only link with life, and my link with death. But tape, alas, is slipping through our fingers into the past.

The things they
used to say about him,
about Gutenberg!
Called him an ignoramus,
egg-head, upstart.
Their fingers were slender,
according to them,
and their nails manicured.
While his were just...
Stumps.
The plebs of print
treading hard on the heels
of the aristocratic culture
of the manuscript.
O how I sympathise,
compelled to learn
digitised computerised
recording and editing.
Will my hands really never
feel again the quiver of
magnetic tape,
frog's back,
puppy's tail?

The laws of physics mean that radio voices are beamed forever into space, so that
if a person has even once been on the air, he is immortal. The hermetically sealed
and soundproofed booths, the control panels, the lack of outside windows make
radio studios like spaceships. And your voice alone is capable of unlocking this
closed space.

So this is the kind of information source you have to handle: a source that
invigorates, pulsates, assuages.

AIR IS FREE

The words "radiation" and "radio" have the same root. Physicists working with
radiation wear special protective clothing. Radio workers have to do without: you
can't put on a lead apron out in space.

I've been a broadcaster for over three decades now, first for the BBC's Russian
Service (Bush House) and then the Russian Service of Radio Free Europe/Radio

Liberty (Munich, Prague). As a rule I'm surrounded by thinking, creative people. Many of them represent the flower of their national culture: outstanding poets, directors, essayists. In "normal" countries a radio station is not the focus of such a gathering of "stars". But I was born in a country which does not count among the "normal". My colleagues are people from other "abnormal" countries, countries where freedom is severely restricted or even completely lacking. The result is that I am surrounded by historical losers, regardless of the personal success any of my colleagues may have achieved. I gaze longingly after my fellow-broadcasters who leave for the "normal" world. The first to go were the Hungarians, Poles and Czechs, then the Estonians, Lithuanians and Latvians. The most recent departees were the Bulgarians and Romanians. Close your eyes for a second and the Ukrainians will have tried to make a break for it, too.

Am I really sentenced to this for life? I feel like a boy who has had to repeat a class, no, repeat a century or maybe even a millennium. What saves me from depression is the language I have discovered and fallen in love with: the language of radio. Radio language is wider, richer, more full-bodied than any spoken tongue. With it you can convey ageing, erotic excitement, the approach of madness, dying. I have no interest in describing culture. But to create and blow culture like glass is thrilling. To me radio is an art form. Radio and poetry live in the same element – air. So for more than thirty years the ground under my feet has been the element of air. A free element.

A WRITER ON THE RADIO

Modern Russian literature owes one to the Western Russian-language radios. For a long time the attitude of Russian writers towards the Western "voices" was one of condescension. The radios took it in their stride. During the Cold War they produced years and cubic miles of free poetry, prose and essays: Pasternak, Grossman, Solzhenitsyn... No radio in a free country could ever have done that: the air has its own language, its own aesthetic. Radio can, when it wants to, be a genre – rich, expressive, original. Sometimes I think I am an acrobat, at others that I am a fresh air salesman. Often I simply despair: working with radio is like heating a house in winter with all the doors and windows open.

Once in the studio I forget I am a writer. Working with sound is no less enthralling than with words. And the image of being an artist shaping sound seems to me much more dramatic than one moulding words: the laws of physics mean that your voice and breath settle out irrevocably into cosmic dust. I published a collection of my broadcasts. I didn't just mechanically reprint the transcripts. The transfer of a broadcast to the printed page requires careful editing. Maybe this is a challenge to physics and the word "irrevocably". There are bound to be losses in this process: without its acoustic colouring, the spoken word becomes etiolated, desiccated on the page. But something does remain, and if that something encapsulates drama, if earth and fate breathe in it, radio becomes literature. I began my radio career like a typical writer: I was patronising towards the broadcast script. But once I discovered the poetry of sound, I started to cheat on literature in the studio. My lyrical hero has been blabbering away in prose and poetry for over three decades. Radio helps atone for lyrical sin. It teaches you to stand modestly to one side, give up your place to those older and younger, nature, musical instruments. People who work with the microphone know what it means to have a compulsion to tell the world, speak out to it. We will not refuse it the right to give tongue, either.

CO-WORKERS

During my career I have worked with two producers: Frank Williams and Marina Smirnova-Frezza. These are both people with especially sensitive ears. Sometimes I would have liked to have blindfolded them: so they wouldn't be distracted.

Frank was very much influenced by crickets, grasshoppers and cicadas. Frank spends the summers on a Greek island where he has a house. Once he brought me back a present, a concerto for cicadas, crickets and bees, composed and performed by the insects of the Aegean. Frank had recorded them while on holiday. He went out into the olive groves at first light, so that the insects' performance would not be spoiled by the extraneous sound; the whoosh of a passing cyclist or the putter of a motorbike. So to create a vehicle for Frank's concerto I wrote a piece called *M. Fabre's Favourites*. I didn't invent Monsieur Fabre, he was a well-known Provençal entomologist. This enabled Frank to let his chirruping friends loose upon the world!

Marina had a profound attachment to dolphins, porpoises and whales. Once I asked her to work on a recording of aquatic voices: they seemed to me insufficiently expressive. Half an hour later I went to the studio and heard this incredible chorus: Marina, eyes closed, was harmonising with a pod of marine mammals. So that this work of art and nature could be released into the cosmos, I wrote a play, *Love On Short Waves*, and since then outer space has been populated with dolphins, porpoises and whales.

Frank is a trifle jealous of Marina: she seems huge to him. While Marina... Marina sailed past the island where Frank spends his summers and didn't hear him. She hears only the noise of the waves.

ALL PRAISE TO THE EAR, OR AN ECLIPSE OF THE MOON

My work means I have to think all the time about the ear. For a normal person hearing is something to be taken for granted, and deafness is a defect, a handicap. In fact, hearing is a divine gift, and one granted to relatively few. There are whole types and sub-types of deaf and even earless animals. They compensate for the absence of hearing by developing a special sensitivity to vibrations. They use their whole body (the belly as opposed to the ear) to listen, as it were. After all sound is also a vibration of the air. Molluscs have a special kind of deafness. But this is a divine irony rather than a divine gift. A mollusc is protected by an exoskeleton, which we usually refer to as a shell. Our ear, on the other hand, is not an internal organ within the skull, but an extrusion of gristle covered in skin which anatomists refer to as the shell of the ear. Yet shells are deaf!

There is a Russian folk expression for people with especially sensitive hearing: "He can hear the grass grow." The Russian verb "to hear", слышать, can be applied to four of the five senses. One – you can hear in the usual meaning of the word (sounds), two – you can "hear" the taste of something ("your tongue isn't a shovel, it hears what's sweet, what's sour"), three – "hear" in the sense of feel ("The girl didn't hear she was pricked and bleeding", Nekrasov), three and a half – simultaneously feel and smell ("You could hear the damp in the air"), four – to smell (hear smells). Plus on top of this you "hear" in the sense of understand ("he doesn't hear Russian") and also obey ("I hear, Sire").

And that's not all. Roland Barthes, the French semiotician and philosopher called the ear the most erotic of human organs in his short study *I Hear and Obey*. He was led to this conclusion by the *Thousand and One Nights,* in which Scheherazade tells Shahryar stories through the night. No, she doesn't seduce him or do a belly dance, she ravishes his ear. Scholars believe that these Arabian stories come from Persian sources, and the last one originates in India. This sounds very plausible: otherwise why would the *Kamasutra* refer to aural (auricular) sex as the "eclipse of the moon". So much poetry is contained in the ear!

A FAILED EXPERIMENT

I keep coming up against the problem of smell and have yet to find a good solution. I once did a programme in Munich on smell. I used a piece by Debussy to go with it, *Les sons et les parfums tournent dans l'air du soir*. The sounds did, indeed, turn, but there was no hint of either perfume or smell for the nose to hear.

Even though the word "ether" has a whiff of alcohol about it, it is hard to appeal to a listener's nose when a programme is in the ether. Poets like to discuss the scent of words. And, yes, words do have a smell. Take a sniff: jasmine, dill, rotting vegetables, orange peel (but not the actual orange), fermenting apple, compost, a wine cork (but not the wine! Wine is colour, deepest red). There are all sorts to choose from: both sweet-smelling and stinky. Poets exploit words' olfactory auras.

Frost again smells of apple.

Mandelshtam doesn't use the word "crunch" here, but it is crunch that marries "apple" and "frost", producing a heady fragrance. In the *Song of Songs* Solomon is less refined when he compares the organ of smell with the source of the aroma: "And the smell of thy nose like apples".

From time to time I have found it possible to convey smell over the radio. For example, Tom Waites' hung-over rasp would convey the rank stench of the alcoholic. But my own programme on smell was a failure. The contributors were fine, very tasty. A Frenchman recalled the old *épiceries* packed with nutmeg, cinnamon, vanilla pods, coffee, cardamom and reduced colonial-imperialist politics to the struggle for spices and flavourings. A Brit recalled the smells of boarding school where young gentlemen were trained to lay down their lives for the Empire: the sickly sweet reek of lavatories overlaid with an all-pervasive odour of boiled cabbage. A Ukrainian poet fought down hatred of his empire to declare: "There is the Russian spirit, there it smells of Rus. Where is there? The Russian spirit blows where it wills!" While one of the last – from the days of *perestroika* – political prisoners from that same empire, an Estonian chimney sweep, compared the compressed stink of Tallinn jail with the pong of Leningrad's Kresty prison and the sterile, morgue-like whiff of the one in Perm. His was a loving stroll down memory lane: "When the warders fry up onion and potatoes next the punishment cell, you can sense every last spare drop of sunflower oil... Or when you catch the scent on the wife of the chief warder, a dentist, in the prison corridor... And toilet soap? It's a waste to wash with it. Better just to sniff it..."

But all this was the descriptive power of words, not radio. In Prague I had another go, to get listeners to hear me with their noses I made a program about cigars. I tried to convey the aroma through thick clouds of jazz, but I don't think it worked this time, either.

A DEFINING IMAGE

I made this discovery in London towards the end of 1979, when I began working for the Russian Service of the BBC.

The first six months were my probationary period and I tried very hard: I came to work at Bush House early, gobbled my lunch, stayed until late. I found writing and translating from English easy, but the technical aspects – recording and editing, mixing speech and music – were a challenge.

One evening I had been recording myself and listening to the result over and over again, when I detected a new timbre in my voice, an intonation that was not quite mine. I was actually taken with the new dimension I discovered in my voice. Where, I wondered, had it come from, this new metropolitan gloss: a combination of Moscow self-assertiveness and Petersburg refinement? Close examination of the tapes revealed the source. In the interests of economy, I had recorded on used tape, and on that particular evening I had picked up reels with the voices of Zinovy, a Muscovite, and Seva, from Petersburg. And by some curious acoustic trick my voice had absorbed, like blotting paper, the voices of my colleagues and acquired a new sound.

From that time on I began squirreling away old recordings of voices that I liked, hiding them in my desk. Thanks to them my voice began to acquire a number of different acoustic personae, not just Zinovy and Seva, but also Sonya, now an elderly lady, who had never lived under the Soviets, and Anatoly Maksimovich with his acquired English theatricality.

My superiors made much of my new-found vocal richness, while my simple-natured colleagues, whose voices I had appropriated, couldn't quite figure out how I'd done it. I was called "a shortwave star", "a wunderkind of the microphone", "the golden voice of the BBC".

I was able to make good use of this experience at Radio Liberty. In their Munich archives I searched out tapes of my favourite broadcasters: Father Alexander, Gayto, Fatima. I never stole old archive recordings. I would make copies and work from them. When they started cutting the budget in the wake of Gorbachev's *perestroika*, some bean-counter suggested wiping old recordings and re-using the tape. Our archive started to dwindle and wither. I was horrified at the prospect of the inevitable consequences that lay in store. Computers came to the rescue: I was able to digitise much of what was left and then transfer it back to tape. To this day my modest flat plays host to mounds of reels. It'll keep me going until retirement.

I am convinced that my radio palimpsest is a hugely important discovery. Around two and a half thousand years ago Plato compared the Sicilian tyrant Dionysius with a palimpsest scroll, since "beneath the gloss of sophistication" he saw Dionysius's essentially despotic nature. Plato's is the first use of palimpsest as metaphor. Coleridge in his notes for *The Wanderings of Cain* writes of the "palimpsest of memory". Coleridge's admirer, Thomas de Quincey in his essay *Suspiria de Profundis,* written hard on the heels of *Confessions of an English Opium Eater,* described the brain as a huge natural palimpsest. De Quincey's essay was translated into French by Baudelaire, and his palimpsest-like brain with its "infinite layers of thought" moved Proust. In our time, Orhan Pamuk has compared Istanbul with a palimpsest, while astronomers refer to the "shadows" of ancient craters on Jupiter's moon, Ganymede, as a palimpsest.

I say there should be no doubt whatsoever: the palimpsest is the defining image for all of life's processes. Are not we all a multi-tiered genetic palimpsest? And does not a jealous lover see in the object of his devotion a palimpsest of others' embraces? O radio! How should I thank you?! Little did I know as I sweated over the tapes smeared with the voices of my colleagues in the studios of the BBC at the close of the second millennium that the secret of life was slipping unhurriedly by on a thin strip of magnetic tape and was carrying, transporting, lofting me up into the stratosphere, from where you see clearly and hear distinctly all intentions, all plans, all meanings.

PERSONALITY AND THE AIR MASS

"Personality" is me, and so can be regarded ironically. That, at least, is how I regard myself. The "air mass" is the material I work with on the radio. One of the materials. And I take this, the "mass", seriously. Its role is crucial in my radio life. From time to time they change my "point of hearing", force me to hear anew, listen closely again and again, correct my audio thoughts.

My latest passion is acoustic archaeology. Let me explain. From time to time I work on programmes about events and people from an age when sound recording equipment had not yet been invented. We can only guess at the character of the sounds and voices that made the air vibrate two hundred or a thousand years ago. It would take people with a very special, I would say, historical sensitivity to recreate the acoustic landscape of times gone by.

One such person was the Dutch cultural historian Johan Huizinga. In *The Autumn of the Middle Ages* he described the motley, vivid contrasts of life at the time, of sounds, too: lepers with rattles, church beggars whining, madmen raving, bells ringing and chains jangling on the legs and necks of miscreants. The early tragedies of Aeschylus also create a soundscape of Athens: the chorus and coryphaeus, the actors literally tear the air of the orchestra apart. Tragedy is a combat of voices, and only secondarily of the hero and the fates. The richest, yet most treacherous, prop in creating an acoustic reconstruction of the past is music.

Spiritual, religious music helps penetrate the hierarchical inner world of a person, but blocks the material "palaeorealism" of life. Some help may be obtained here from "low" musical styles.

Getting back to the term "acoustic archaeology", one of the key terms in classic archaeology is "excavation". What can a broadcaster "excavate"? In my view, it is most like the work of a poet. Pasternak writes about the air "dug over with shouts". Yes, once attuned, cleansed, the hearing can "excavate" prayers addressed to God or the forces of nature, deathbed groans, aubades and serenades, the agonies of cattle being taken to slaughter, the rustle of angels' wings. No less intently than poets, spiritualist mediums hearkened and hearken still to the air. But for radio, the voices of the spirits are deprived of meaning, because spirits lack the necessary apparatus of the throat, meaning vocal chords, they lack the throat itself, the tongue, the lips, the soft tissue. The classic examples of vocal mediums are Job, Socrates, Joan of Arc who heard voices and even whole conversations. Alas, we can only read accounts of this or consider these cases theoretically. What is more, modern medicine describes these phenomena as deviations from the psychological norm. Psychiatrists think Socrates and Joan of Arc suffered from acute paranoid schizophrenia. That is where acoustic "excavations" can lead the unwitting enthusiast!

All the same, I have evidence of a direct link between archaeology and electromagnetic waves. Marine archaeology, a sub-type of classic archaeology, makes extensive use of sonar and echo-locators. They are used to obtain an acoustic image of a submerged vessel, an acoustic "photograph" of the sea bed or drowned city. So, I will not be surprised if one day I receive visit from a marine archaeologist with an audio album of Atlantis.

To be continued

INTRODUCTION
TO JENŐ DSIDA'S POEMS

George Gömöri

Jenő Dsida was born in 1907 in Szatmárnémeti (today Satu Mare in Romania). He began writing in his early youth and his first poems were published in the children's magazine *Cimbora* ("My Pal") edited by Elek Benedek. His first book of poetry *Leselkedő magány* ("Lurking Solitude") was published in 1928 – by that time Dsida was a student of Law at Kolozsvár (today Cluj–Napoca in Romania). He did not finish his legal studies but took up journalism, becoming the technical editor of *Keleti újság*, a Hungarian-language daily published at Kolozsvár. At the same time his poems were published in Transylvanian literary magazines such as *Pásztortűz* and the much-vaunted *Erdélyi Helikon*. Although with the collection *Nagycsütörtök* ("Maundy Thursday") Dsida made his name as one of the best Hungarian poets in Transylvania, it was his posthumous book of poetry *Angyalok citeráján* ("On the Zither of Angels") which confirmed his place amongst the true masters of the Hungarian language. He died very young, at the age of 31 – we commemorate the seventy-fifth anniversary of his death this year.

Dsida was born with a heart condition and a leading motif of his poetry from the beginning is not so much "lurking solitude" as sudden death embedded in his body cells, ready to attack at any time. He expresses the awareness of death in two different ways: some of his poems such as "The Poem of Darkness" or "Farewell to the Condemned" are imbued with the fear of death, sometimes presented through images of natural decay or condensed in a great metaphor. In his brilliantly rhyming poem "Serenade for Ilonka" Dsida recalls the memory of a young girl snatched away by death at an early age, turning this event into a metaphysical adventure complete with a kind of poetic resurrection. The motto of this poem comes from "Annabel Lee", a similar poem by Edgar Allen Poe and the melody of this beguiling and enchanting poem certainly influenced Dsida.

Denial of the fear of death and a strong confirmation of life are also an inspiration for Dsida: see the charming long poem "Why Did the Angels Prostrate Themselves in Front of Viola?", also the more descriptive "Afternoon Roaming with My Beloved Dog" written in flowing hexameters. His world-view is manifest in both poems: it is a "Franciscan" version of Christianity based on solidarity with the poor and

Jenő Dsida

understanding for people living on the margins of society. Dsida wrote only a few religious poems, amongst which is the memorable "Maundy Thursday" *(Nagycsütörtök)* recalling the suffering Jesus in the Garden of Gethsemane, though it is more about the loneliness of an individual belonging to the ethnic minority in Romania alone in the stuffy waiting-room of a Transylvanian railway station at night.

Lately Dsida's long poem "Psalmus Hungaricus" has become popular in Hungary. This poem was written in the mid-thirties of the last century as a reaction to new laws which drastically restricted the rights of Hungarians in the Kingdom of Romania. It was not published in Dsida's lifetime, partly because (we know this from a reliable source) the poet was not entirely happy with the first version of the poem and partly because of a few lines which could have been deemed provocatively nationalistic. While "Psalmus" is an important poem, it is not amongst the best poetic achievements of Dsida, considering that he was never anti-Romanian and during his last fatal illness was considering the translation of the entire oeuvre of the Romanian classical poet, Eminescu, into Hungarian.

Let me add here a personal note: I was still in my teens in secondary school when I first came across this outstanding Transylvanian poet, marginalised and largely ignored by communist critics. In the summer of 1956, with three years of philological studies behind me at the Eötvös Loránd University (ELTE) of Budapest I visited Cluj/Kolozsvár to do some research for a few weeks on Dsida. Thanks to serendipity I found a few unknown poems by him which were then published in September 1956 in the local Hungarian-language literary weekly *Útunk*, accompanied with an article "Awakening Jenő Dsida" by the editor Zoltán

Panek. This started a debate about the rehabilitation of Dsida, the short term-results of which were negative for Panek and other supporters of the poet, but on the long run it prepared the ground for an incomplete yet generous selection of Dsida's poems ten years later, in 1966. The publication of the *Collected Poems* of Jenő Dsida however had to wait until 2012 when, thanks to the perseverance of Gusztáv Láng they finally reached the Hungarian reader.

Jenő Dsida

MAUNDY THURSDAY

No connection. The train would be six hours
late, it was announced, and that Maundy Thursday
I sat for six hours in the airless dark
of the waiting room of Kocsárd's tiny station.
My soul was heavy and my body broken –
I felt like one who, on a secret journey,
sets out in darkness, summoned by the stars
on fateful earth, braving yet fleeing doom;
whose nerves are so alert that he can sense
enemies, far off, tracking him by stealth.
Outside the window engines rumbled by
and dense smoke like the wing of a huge bat
brushed my face. I felt dull horror, gripped
by a deep bestial fear. I looked around:
it would have been so good to speak a little
to close friends, a few words to men you trust,
but there was only damp night, dark and chill,
Peter was now asleep, and James and John
asleep, and Matthew, all of them asleep…
Thick beads of cold sweat broke out on my brow
and then streamed down over my crumpled face.

A CONFESSION

Where I live is like an island.
Each day what can I do
but kneel – preoccupied
by nothing except you?
It may be the sun cools,

it may be the moon will fall,
this resonant otherworld
dissolves me, absorbs me whole.
It has sweet fragrances,
the light has its own tricks,
the laws governing it
are happy as they are strict.
What elsewhere would be measured
by the tick of a small clock
here by the steady throbbing
in your breast is marked;
you speak and each soft word
that, dreamily, you yield
becomes a silver flower
set in a blue field;
and your sigh is the wind
stirring in my hair,
and your face has the moon's glow,
and your face has the sun's glare.

LAST YEAR'S LOVE

A memory that glitters,
though sometimes too it glares
at my pallid face, as I look
back into past years.
It was bright as a star is bright,
like fire it gave off heat,
also as white as snow
and, like honey, sweet.
I see its gleam at times
but the torment has now ceased;
it's a cool, friendly hand –
I feel its light caress.
It has fallen like a star,
it has gone out like fire,
it's melted as snow melts
and the sweetness has turned sour.

THE POEM OF DARKNESS

Once more, the vigil season!
Broad pen-strokes on my sheet look grim.
Night's rust-juice floods the gardens,
by six full to the brim.
Damp oozes from the mouldering trees,
you muse on how much time
you've left. Your foot stops dead, in fear
of stumbling into a tomb...
But tell me: have you ever let
a snow-white sugar-cube soak up
dark liquid, dipped in the bitter night
of coffee in its cup?
Or watched how the dense liquid,
so surely, so insidiously,
will seep up through the white cube's
pure, crystalline body?
Just so the night seeps into you,
slowly rising, the smells
of night and of the grave all through
your veins, fibres, cells,
until one dank brown evening,
so steeped in it, you melt and sink –
to sweeten, for some unknown god,
his dark and bitter drink.

Translated by George Gömöri and Clive Wilmer

OUR AUTHORS

PÉTER ÁKOS BOD (Szigetvár, 1951) economist, university professor. He worked in economic research at the Institute of Planning, Budapest, taught economics in Budapest and in the US before 1989. He was Minister of Industry and Trade between 1990 and 1991, and Governor of the Hungarian National Bank between 1991 and 1994. In 1995–1998, he was member of the Board at the European Bank for Reconstruction and Development (London), representing East Central European countries. At present, he is director of the Institute of Economics at Corvinus University of Budapest. He is vice chairman of the Hungarian Economic Society, sits on editorial boards of Hungarian journals (inc. this *Review*). His major publications include *A vállalkozó állam* (Entrepreneurial State) – 1987; *A pénz világa* (The World of Money) – 2001; *Gazdaságpolitika* (Economic Policy) – 2002; *Közgazdaságtan* (Economics) – 2006.

ENIKŐ BOLLOBÁS (Budapest, 1952) is Professor and Chair of the Department of American Studies, ELTE, Budapest. A Doctor of the Hungarian Academy of Letters and Sciences (D.Litt./D.Sc.), she has published five books, including a monograph on the American poet Charles Olson (Twayne), a history of American literature (Osiris), a study on subjectivity in literature (Peter Lang), and last year a book on the tropes of performative subjectivity in American and Hungarian literature (Balassi). Bollobás has been

visiting professor and invited speaker at various universities, including the University of Oregon, the University of Iowa, Yale, Berkeley, Stanford, Georgetown, UCSD and Cambridge University (England). Her opinion pieces appeared in *The Washington Post* and *The International Herald Tribune*, and were incorporated into the *Congressional Record* of the US Congress.

GEORGE GÖMÖRI (Budapest, 1934) has been living in England since November 1956. After studies in Oxford, he taught at the University of California (Berkeley), researched at Harvard. From 1969 to 2001 he taught at the University of Cambridge. He published many books on Polish and Hungarian literature, also 12 books of poetry in Hungarian and two in English. He is a member of the Polish Academy of Arts and Sciences (Cracow).

NORBERT HAKLIK (Ózd, 1976), writer and critic, studied Hungarian and English literature and linguistics in Budapest. He is the author of two short story compilations (*A Mennybemeneteli Iroda* [Salvation Agency], 1998, 2013; *Világvége Gömörlúcon* [The World's End in Gömörlúc], 2001), a novel (*Big Székely Só* [Big Szekler Show], 2006), and several translations from English into Hungarian. His latest work *Egy Duna-regény anatómiája* (The anatomy of a Danube-novel), 2013 is a set of literary essays that entirely focuses on Thomas Kabdebo's novel trilogy

Danubius Danubia, just like the work published in the present issue of *Hungarian Review*. Haklik currently lives in Brno (the Czech Republic), with his wife and daughter, and – besides his 9-to-5 job as a manager for a global IT company – is working on a new short story collection.

OTTO HIERONYMI (Budapest, 1938), economist, is Former Head (1995-2006) of the Program of International Relations, Webster University, Geneva. In 1970–1994 he was Senior Economist at Battelle Geneva Research Centers. 1966–1970 he was an International Economist with Morgan Guaranty Trust in New York. He earned his Licence and Doctorate in international relations and economics at the Graduate Institute of International Relations (University of Geneva). He was Economic Adviser to Prime Minister József Antall (1990–1993) also working on committees on the Bank Reform and a new strategy for growth (GAM – 1991–1992). In 1989 he was the Secretary of the Expert Group on the International Debt issue (Languetin Commission) appointed by the Swiss Federal Government. His publications include among others: *Economic Policies for the New Hungary: Proposals for a Coherent Approach (1990 – the so-called "Battelle Report")*; *Globalization and the Reform of the International Banking and Monetary System* (Editor, 2009); *Global Challenges, the Atlantic Community and the Outlook for International Order*; (Editor, 2004); *Wilhelm Röpke, the Social Market Economy and Today's Domestic and International Order* (Editor, 2002); *Renewing the Western Community: the Challenge for the EU, Europe and Japan* (Editor, 2011 forthcoming). He is currently working on the manuscript of *Regime Change: the Economic Policies of the Antall Government*.

GÉZA JESZENSZKY (Budapest, 1941), D. Phil., historian, graduated from Eötvös Loránd University in Budapest, teaching at Corvinus University, Budapest at present. He taught history of Central Europe at U.C. Santa Barbara in 1984–88, and has lectured at numerous universities and institutions in the US and Europe. He was Foreign Minister of Hungary in the first non-Communist government (1990–94), and Ambassador to the United States of America in 1998–2004. He is an avid skier and hiker. He is the author of numerous publications on history and foreign policy, his latest book in English is *Post-Communist Europe and its National/Ethnic Problems*. He is an editorial adviser for *Hungarian Review*.

GEORGE JONAS (Budapest, 1935) is a Hungarian-born Canadian writer, poet and journalist, describing himself as a classical liberal. His works include *Vengeance* (1984), the story of an Israeli operation to kill the terrorists responsible for the 1972 Munich massacre. The book was adapted for two films, *Sword of Gideon* (1986) and *Munich* (2005). Jonas worked as a radio producer in Budapest before escaping to the West after the fall of the 1956 Hungarian Revolution. He worked for the Canadian Broadcasting Corporation as a script editor and producer. He worked as a columnist for the *Toronto Sun* from 1981 to 2001, when he moved to the *National Post* where he remains a regular contributor. He has written 16 books, one play and two operas. His latest book, *The Jonas Variations* (2012), includes his translations from the classical poems of many languages.

AMBRUS MISKOLCZY (Marosvásárhely – Turgu Mures, Romania, 1947) is a Hungarian historian born and educated in Transylvania. He is a Member of the Hungarian Academy of Sciences, and one of the editors of the *New International Journal for Romanian Studies*. As Chair of the Department of Romanian Philology at Eötvös Loránd University in Budapest, he has done extensive research on the co-habitation of Romanians, Hungarians and Saxons in Transylvania, and published studies on mentality, with special regard to the culture of the middle classes and to national myths.

JOHN O'SULLIVAN (Liverpool, 1942) is editor-at-large of *National Review* in New York where he served as Editor-in-Chief for ten years. He was a Special Adviser to Prime Minister Margaret Thatcher in Downing Street and later assisted her in the writing of her two volumes of memoirs. He has held a wide variety of senior editorial positions in the media on both sides of the Atlantic. He is the founder and co-chairman of the Atlantic Initiative, an international bipartisan organisation dedicated to reinvigorating and expanding the Atlantic community of democracies, launched at the Congress of Prague in May 1996 by President

Václav Havel and Lady Thatcher. His book, *The President, the Pope, and the Prime Minister* (on Pope John Paul II, President Reagan and Prime Minister Thatcher), was published in Hungarian, too, in 2010. Until 2011, he was the Executive Editor of Radio Free Europe and Radio Liberty in Prague.

TIBOR PETHŐ (Budapest, 1973), journalist, graduated in History at Pázmány Péter Catholic University in Piliscsaba. After graduation he taught at grammar schools. He is employed by the Budapest daily *Magyar Nemzet,* which was founded by his great-grandfather Sándor Pethő on the eve of the Second World War. He writes theatre criticism for the daily edition and documentary features for the weekend magazine, specialising in the hidden history of totalitarian regimes in Hungary. He lives with his family in Budapest.

JAAP SCHOLTEN (Enschede, 1963) studied Industrial Design at the Technical University in Delft, Graphic Design at the Willem de Kooning Academy of Arts in Rotterdam (BA), and Social Anthropology at the Central European University in Budapest (MA). He has published seven books: collections of short stories and three novels. His latest novel, *De wet van Spengler* (AtlasContact, 2008), was chosen "novel of the year" in the Netherlands. His latest book, *Kameraad Baron* (AtlasContact, 2010) is the winner of the Libris History Prize 2011. His novels and short stories are translated into German, French, Hungarian, Croatian and his last book *Kameraad Baron* into English. In 2011

Scholten created and presented a six-part television series for the VPRO about hidden worlds in Central and Eastern Europe. He lives in Budapest since 2003.

İLTER TURAN is a professor of political science at Istanbul's Bilgi University, where he also served as president between 1998–2001. His previous employment included professorships at Koç University (1993–1998) and Istanbul University (1964–1993), where he also served as the chair of the International Relations Department (1987–1993), and the director of the Center for the Study of the Balkans and the Middle East (1985–1993). Dr Turan is the past president of the Turkish Political Science Association and has been a member of the Executive Committee and a vice president of the International Political Science Association (2000–2006). He is a frequent commentator on Turkish politics on TV and newspapers.

ROGER VERNON SCRUTON (Manchester, 1944) is a conservative English philosopher and writer. He is the author of over 30 books, including *Art and Imagination* (1974), *Sexual Desire* (1986), *The Aesthetics of Music* (1997), *A Political Philosophy: Arguments for Conservatism* (2006) and *Green Philosophy* (2012). He has also written several novels and two operas. Scruton was a lecturer and professor of aesthetics at Birkbeck College, London, from 1971 to 1992. In 1982 he helped found *The Salisbury Review*, a conservative political journal, which he edited for 18 years. Since 1992 he has held part-time positions at Boston University, the American Enterprise Institute in Washington, DC, and the University of St Andrews. He also founded the Claridge Press in 1987, and sits on the editorial board of the *British Journal of Aesthetics*. He serves in addition as a member of the International Advisory Board of the Centre for European Renewal.

Sponsored by:

Polgári
Magyarországért
Alapítvány

Foundation for a Civic Hungary   Batthyány Lajos Foundation

HUNGARIAN REVIEW is an affiliate of the bi-monthly journal
Magyar Szemle, published since 1991, edited by Gyula Kodolányi

HUNGARIAN REVIEW is published by BL Nonprofit Kft.
Budapest, 1067, Eötvös u. 24., Hungary
Publisher: György Granasztói

Editorial office: Budapest, 1067, Eötvös u. 24., Hungary
Phone: +36 1 706 8866
Fax: +36 1 706 8867
Editorial Manager: Ildikó Geiger
E-mail: hungarianreview@hungarianreview.com
Online edition: www.hungarianreview.com

ISSN 2062-2031

Design and Typography: Flagrans, Budapest
Printed by Pauker Nyomda

To subscribe to Hungarian Review, please write to:
Violetta Ibolya Dán, Circulation and Subscriptions Manager
E-mail: subscriptions@hungarianreview.com
or use our PayPal service on our website

Hungarian Review annual subscriptions for six issues, including postage:
• Hungary: 6000 HUF • Great Britain: £48 • Europe: €60 • US and Overseas: $84
Copies of HR can be purchased through Amazon.com
It can be read as an E-Book at www.ceeol.com

Bank transfers: BL Nonprofit Kft. Erste Bank Budapest
HU86 11600006-00000000-44612755
SWIFT code: GIBAHUHB

In Hungary, subscriptions are also available through Magyar Posta.